Export Consortia in Developing Countries

Fabio Antoldi
Daniele Cerrato
Donatella Depperu

Export Consortia in Developing Countries

Successful Management
of Cooperation Among SMEs

Fabio Antoldi
Università Cattolica del Sacro Cuore
Department of Economic and Social Sciences
Via Emilia Parmense 84
29122 Piacenza
Italy
fabio.antoldi@unicatt.it

Prof. Donatella Depperu
Università Cattolica del Sacro Cuore
Department of Economic and Social Sciences
Via Emilia Parmense 84
29122 Piacenza
Italy
donatella.depperu@unicatt.it

Daniele Cerrato
Università Cattolica del Sacro Cuore
Department of Economic and Social Sciences
Via Emilia Parmense 84
29122 Piacenza
Italy
daniele.cerrato@unicatt.it

ISBN 978-3-642-24878-8   e-ISBN 978-3-642-24879-5
DOI 10.1007/978-3-642-24879-5
Springer Heidelberg Dordrecht London New York

Library of Congress Control Number: 2011945092

© Springer-Verlag Berlin Heidelberg 2011
This work is subject to copyright. All rights are reserved, whether the whole or part of the material is concerned, specifically the rights of translation, reprinting, reuse of illustrations, recitation, broadcasting, reproduction on microfilm or in any other way, and storage in data banks. Duplication of this publication or parts thereof is permitted only under the provisions of the German Copyright Law of September 9, 1965, in its current version, and permission for use must always be obtained from Springer. Violations are liable to prosecution under the German Copyright Law.
The use of general descriptive names, registered names, trademarks, etc. in this publication does not imply, even in the absence of a specific statement, that such names are exempt from the relevant protective laws and regulations and therefore free for general use.

Printed on acid-free paper

Springer is part of Springer Science+Business Media (www.springer.com)

Preface

Small and medium-sized enterprises (SMEs) are highly significant in both developed and developing countries as a proportion of the total number of firms, for the contribution they can make to employment, and for their ability to develop innovation.

The internationalization of SMEs is an increasing global trend and attracts the interest of not only academic researchers, but also policy-makers, as it is seen as an important means of enhancing the long-term growth and profitability of SMEs. Governments are interested in setting up support programmes which enable firms to increase their export sales, given the positive effects that increasing exports has on the economic growth and competitiveness of countries.

SMEs suffer from a number of major internal barriers to export related to their limited resources and lack of competences necessary to meet the challenges of the new business environment. This is particularly true of SMEs in developing countries, where relatively few entrepreneurs have international experience or a high level of management education. Compared to those in developed countries, firms in developing economies have fewer managerial resources and fewer private or public support services. Both these factors negatively affect their ability to go international.

It is widely acknowledged that firms are able to increase their export potential by leveraging on networks or collaborative strategies. Export consortia represent specific network arrangements, based on domestic collaborative relationships, which are well-suited to the characteristics of SMEs. Export consortia generally involve SMEs which are characterized by complementary and mutually-enhancing offers, and may be sales- or promotion-oriented. Consortia of SMEs can facilitate solutions to export problems and enable the loosening of the constraints related to the investments needed to penetrate foreign markets. However, the successful management of cooperation among SMEs in the form of export consortia makes it necessary to pay careful attention to the distinctive features of these networks.

Although the importance of cooperation for the international competitiveness of small firms in both industrialized countries and developing countries is widely acknowledged, the interest of academic research in export consortia has until recently been very limited. They continue to be almost completely unexplored in academic publications. Export consortia appear to be one area of professional practice that management research has not been able to analyze, despite its economic relevance and social implications. This publication aims to fill this gap in management literature.

The book analyzes export consortia from the strategic management perspective. It builds on an empirical analysis of nine export consortia promoted by UNIDO (United Nations Industrial Development Organization) in developing countries between 2004 and 2007: four in Peru, three in Morocco, and one each in Tunisia and Uruguay. Besides reviewing the academic literature and discussing models for the management of export consortia, the book is based heavily on actual export consortium experiences, in order to combine a rigorous research approach with a more pragmatic view of the phenomenon.

The material presented here will be of interest to a variety of different readers.

Scholars in the field of management represent our primary target. We include a literature review which combines the topics of SME internationalization, strategic networks and alliances, and the issues which relate specifically to SME alliances in the form of export consortia.

Entrepreneurs and executives involved in the internationalization processes of SMEs will find useful business models and management tools for the successful design and implementation of export consortia. This is also the case for management consultants who support the international expansion of SMEs, and whose role is often crucial in the start-up of export consortia.

Insights into the functioning of export consortia may also be of interest to policy-makers and institutions that develop support programmes for the growth of SMEs in developing countries. Given the relevance of internationalization as a driver of competitiveness at both micro and macro level, policy-makers from developing countries are increasingly interested in setting up appropriate systems of incentives and support services that can enable firms to grow and be successful in foreign markets. For this reason, there is considerable benefit to be gained from a deeper understanding of export consortia and a better comprehension of the mechanisms that favour the successful management of cooperation among SMEs.

The book is divided into five chapters. In Chap. 1 we provide an overview of the different research streams that have addressed the issue of SME internationalization. Building on a review of export literature and studies on SME internationalization, we discuss the factors affecting the international development of SMEs as well as the barriers which block or hinder them from initiating or increasing export activities. We then focus on SMEs in developing countries. Empirical evidence from modern global manufacturing systems and increasing economic integration shows that the internationalization pathways of SMEs from developing countries may be more heterogeneous than those assumed by traditional models, which were defined in the context of mature developed economies.

Chapter 2 deals with networks. Network-based research shows that the internationalization process of firms is driven largely by network relationships. Joining a network can be even more important for SMEs, as they face a variety of internal constraints due mainly to a lack of financial and managerial resources. In this chapter we introduce the main concepts related to inter-firm networks and focus on the strategic issues involved in building a network of SMEs. After defining strategic networks and presenting the different types, we analyze how a network may become an additional source of competitive advantage for the small firms involved. We then discuss to what extent trust among entrepreneurs is able to consolidate and ensure the continuity of the network. Finally, we analyze the crucial role that third parties, acting as 'network facilitators', may play in promoting and strengthening relationships among entrepreneurs.

Chapter 3 focuses on export consortia, which are a particular form of inter-firm network, based on domestic collaborative relationships, and dedicated to fostering the internationalization of SMEs. In this chapter, we present different types of export consortia, describing their features as well as highlighting their advantages and disadvantages compared to other kinds of network. From a dynamic perspective, the possible life-cycle of a consortium is also described. Data on the diffusion of export consortia are also presented, as well as a description of the UNIDO programme to assist developing countries and transition economies in establishing export consortia.

In Chapter 4, we show the empirical evidence which forms the basis of the book. Our analysis covers nine export consortia supported by UNIDO in developing countries between 2004 and 2007. After detailing the objectives and methodology of the empirical investigation, we present a concise version of the nine case histories compiled during the research in order to describe the main features of each of the export consortia analyzed: origins, membership, strategies and goals, governance structures, organization and management systems.

In Chapter 5, a framework for analyzing the management of export consortia is described along with several tools designed to enable firms to formulate and implement effective consortium strategies and monitor performance. Our framework focuses on six activities related to the setting-up and management of export consortia: managing the strategic alignment of member firms; formulating a consortium strategy; designing the consortium's organizational structure; designing leadership and governance systems; leveraging on strategic resources and distinctive competences, and measuring consortium performance.

This book is the result of a research program developed jointly by the authors, who contributed equally to both the development of the core ideas and the research activity. Primary responsibility for the writing of the different sections was divided as follows:

Fabio Antoldi wrote Chap. 2, Chap. 4 (Sects. 4.6, 4.7, 4.8, 4.9, 4.10), Chap. 5 (Sects. 5.4, 5.6, and 5.7); Daniele Cerrato: Chap. 1, Chap. 4 (Sects. 4.1, 4.2, 4.3, 4.4, and 4.5), Chap. 5 (Sects. 5.3 and 5.5); Donatella Depperu: Chap. 3, Chap. 5 (Sects. 5.1 and 5.2).

Export consortia are likely to become more widespread in the future. A more in-depth knowledge of the important issues related to the strategic management of export consortia is therefore fundamental in order to be able to design and manage these network arrangements effectively, and to successfully manage cooperation among SMEs.

Acknowledgments

The authors would like to express their gratitude to the staff of the 'Cluster and Business Linkages Unit' of the Private Sector Development Branch of UNIDO, and in particular to Fabio Russo, Senior Industrial Development Officer and Export Consortia Programme Manager; Ebe Muschialli, UNIDO Export Consortia International Expert in Morocco and Gilles Galtieri, Export Consortia Development Consultant, for their invaluable support and insightful comments, and to the officers and consultants of UNIDO involved in promoting consortia in Uruguay, Peru, Morocco, and Tunisia, for their contribution to the infield analysis. All the materials presented in this publication, however, including any errors or misinterpretations, remain the responsibility of the authors and should not be considered as necessarily reflecting the views or carrying the endorsement of UNIDO. This publication has benefited from the financial support of the Università Cattolica del Sacro Cuore in 2011.

Contents

1 **Internationalization of Small and Medium-Sized Enterprises** 1
   1.1 SMEs and International Markets 1
   1.2 SME Internationalization: Contributions from Different
        Theoretical Perspectives 2
        1.2.1 The Incremental Approach to Internationalization 2
        1.2.2 The 'Born Global' Phenomenon 3
        1.2.3 A Resource-Based View of Internationalization 4
        1.2.4 Internationalization from a Network-Based Perspective . 5
   1.3 Barriers to SME Export: A Classification 6
        1.3.1 Internal Barriers 8
        1.3.2 External Barriers 9
   1.4 Firm Resources, Management Characteristics and SME
        Exporting Activity 10
   1.5 The Characteristics of Developing Countries 13
   1.6 Patterns of SME International Expansion 15
   References 17

2 **Strategic Networks, Trust and the Competitive Advantage
of SMEs** 23
   2.1 SME Attitude Towards Cooperation 23
   2.2 Defining Strategic Networks of SMEs 24
   2.3 SMEs and Competitiveness: The Relational Perspective 28
   2.4 The Relevance of Social Capital Within the Network 30
   2.5 Networks as Sources of Competitive Advantage 31
   2.6 Trust as a Requirement for Building Successful
        SME Networks 33
   2.7 The Role of 'Network Facilitators': An Interpretative
        Framework 35
   References 40

3 **Export Consortia: Types and Characteristics** 45
   3.1 Export Consortia: An Overview 45
   3.2 Features, Strengths and Weaknesses of Export Consortia 47
   3.3 Export Consortia from a Dynamic Perspective: The Lifecycle
        of the Firm-Consortium Relationship 50

	3.4	The Diffusion of Export Consortia in Developed Countries	52
	3.5	Export Consortia in Developing Countries	54
	3.6	The Experience of the United Nations Industrial Development Organization in Promoting SME Export Consortia	55
	References		57
4	**Empirical Analysis of Nine Export Consortia of SMEs in Morocco, Tunisia, Peru and Uruguay**		59
	4.1	The Field Research: Data Collection and Analysis	59
	4.2	Mosaic (Morocco)	62
	4.3	Vitargan (Morocco)	64
	4.4	Travel Partners (Morocco)	66
	4.5	Get'IT (Tunisia)	67
	4.6	Muyu (Peru)	69
	4.7	Peruvian Bio Consortia (Peru)	71
	4.8	ACMC (Peru)	72
	4.9	Ande Natura (Peru)	74
	4.10	Phyto Uruguay (Uruguay)	76
	References		77
5	**The Management of Export Consortia: A Pragmatic Approach**		79
	5.1	A Framework for the Analysis of Export Consortium Management	79
	5.2	Managing the Strategic Alignment of Member Firms	82
	5.3	Formulating Consortium Strategy	88
	5.4	Designing the Organizational Structure	94
	5.5	Leveraging on Strategic Resources and Competences	98
	5.6	Enforcing Corporate Governance and Leadership	106
	5.7	Measuring Consortium Performance	111
	References		117
6	**Conclusions**		119

List of Authors

Fabio Antoldi is Associate Professor of Business Strategy at the Università Cattolica del Sacro Cuore, Piacenza, Italy

Daniele Cerrato is Assistant Professor of International Business at the Università Cattolica del Sacro Cuore, Piacenza, Italy

Donatella Depperu is Professor of Business Administration and Srategic Management at the Università Cattolica del Sacro Cuore, Piacenza, Italy

Internationalization of Small and Medium-Sized Enterprises

1.1 SMEs and International Markets

Technological improvements, more efficient international communications and transportation, regional economic integration and a number of trade agreements have dramatically changed the international business environment and contributed to the growth of international trade. At a macro level, increasing exports is considered to have positive effects on economic growth and employment levels. At a micro level, exporting allows firms to pursue growth opportunities, diversify business risks and increase profits (Leonidou and Katsikeas 1996; Ramaseshan and Soutar 1996).

As international markets are becoming increasingly integrated and interdependent, virtually all firms, regardless of their size, industry or country of origin, need to develop a strategic response to international competition. Small and medium-sized enterprises (SMEs) have become aware of the importance of internationalization as a means of enhancing their long-term growth, profitability and chances of survival (Morgan and Katsikeas 1997).

Exporting is generally the first stage in the process of internationalization and, particularly among SMEs, is considered the most common entry mode into a foreign market as it involves a lower business risk, less commitment of resources and greater flexibility than joint ventures or foreign direct investments (FDIs).

Factors affecting firms' export behaviour have been studied by researchers from the fields of economics, marketing and management. Renewed interest in the topic is a result of the increasing role of emerging economies in export trade (Singh 2009). In a global world, and especially in developing countries, the number of small firms engaged in export activities is increasing as a result of greater subcontracting between SMEs and foreign firms. Global competition represents not only an opportunity, but also a threat. As SMEs are no longer protected from foreign competition, they need to go international in order to remain competitive in their local markets. SMEs therefore need to overcome their limited experience in international markets. This is especially true in the case of SMEs in developing countries, who are generally less experienced in exporting, especially to customers in the developed world. SMEs suffer from a number of major internal barriers relating to their limited resources and capabilities.

Much of the literature concerning the internationalization of firms has traditionally focused on multinational enterprises (MNEs) or large, well-established firms in developed economies (Buckley and Casson 1976; Dunning 1981; Hymer 1976). However, the internationalization of SMEs is an increasing global trend in both developed and developing countries, and has not only attracted the interest of academic researchers, but also raised questions among policy-makers. Governments are interested in setting up appropriate systems of incentives and support services that can enable firms to grow and be successful in foreign markets. Government agencies and related organizations can help firms participate in international fairs and facilitate solutions to export problems. The enhancement of a firm's export activity is a big challenge in developing countries. The institutional environment of these countries is quite different from what is often found in developed countries, in terms of governmental support, infrastructure and regulation.

In addition, it is increasingly acknowledged that firms can develop their export potential by leveraging on networks or collaborative strategies. Combining resources, knowledge and experience can lead to more rapid internationalization. Export consortia are typical examples of such collaborative arrangements. Using interfirm collaborations, SMEs can exploit and integrate complementary resources and competences, jointly promote investments in shared resources, increase their responsiveness to more sophisticated demand standards and, as a result, achieve higher export levels (Mesquita and Lazzarini 2008; Schmitz 1995; Tallman et al. 2004).

1.2 SME Internationalization: Contributions from Different Theoretical Perspectives

Firms operating in foreign countries have higher costs than local firms due to factors such as lack of local information and market knowledge and unfamiliarity with the local culture and business environment (Hymer 1976). This disadvantage is known as the 'liability of foreignness' (Zaheer 1995). For this reason, firms need to accumulate and leverage on their firm-specific advantages in order to expand abroad and gain a superior competitive position over local firms.

Building on different theoretical perspectives, the internationalization literature highlights the factors affecting the foreign expansion of SMEs, and shows how they can overcome the liability/disadvantages associated with it.

1.2.1 The Incremental Approach to Internationalization

The Uppsala model (or stage theory) is one of the best known models of business internationalization. It was developed by Johanson and Vahlne (1977) on the basis of their analysis of four Swedish export companies. They introduced the concept of internationalization as an incremental process, and argued that firms gradually go through different stages of international development, which reflect their increasing knowledge and commitment to foreign operations (Johanson and Wiedersheim-Paul 1975; Johanson and Vahlne 1977).

The model suggests that firms initially enter foreign markets that are comparatively well-known and similar to their own in terms of economic development, political system, culture, business practices, legal environment, religion, language and education, and then gradually progress to markets that are more 'psychically' distant. Psychic distance refers to all those factors preventing or disturbing the flow of information between firm and host market, such as differences in language, culture, political system, level of industrial development, etc. (Johanson and Wiedersheim-Paul 1975).

The Uppsala model views a firm's experiential knowledge as the main factor in reducing the uncertainty associated with foreign expansion (Andersson 2004) and in driving both geographical scope and changes in entry modes. As a firm's market knowledge increases, it enters markets that are increasingly 'psychically' distant and, within them, progressively modifies its entry modes from exporting to the greater involvement required by alliances and subsidiaries. Market knowledge, which can be gained from experience with foreign activities, is therefore the key factor influencing the time and direction of international development. Only experience can reduce the uncertainty associated with international expansion and remove the principal obstacle to it (Leonidou and Katsikeas 1996). From this perspective, the internationalization of a firm is described as a process of increasing a firm's international involvement through gradual learning and development of market knowledge.

The stage model provides some guidelines for the internationalization of SMEs and emphasizes two key points:
- the knowledge of foreign markets as a key driver of internationalization;
- the importance of the learning processes associated with internationalization.

However, in the modern global economy, the universal applicability of the slow, incremental model of internationalization has been questioned (Bell 1995; Bell et al. 2003). Furthermore, it does not seem to have sufficient explanatory power in relation to the realities of developing countries where SMEs may follow a different foreign expansion route from the conventional model of internationalization in developed countries (see Sect. 1.6).

1.2.2 The 'Born Global' Phenomenon

Empirical evidence about 'born globals' – companies that are international from their inception or shortly afterwards – has challenged the incremental view of internationalization (Knight and Cavusgil 1996; Madsen and Servais 1997). Firms which are international from the beginning of their activity are also known as 'global start-ups' (Oviatt and McDougall 1995), 'early internationalizing firms' or 'international new ventures' (McDougall et al. 1994; Oviatt and McDougall 1994). Many born global firms are rather small. They develop entrepreneurial strategies to exploit international opportunities simultaneously in a variety of markets. Born global firms internationalize rapidly by developing international networks, relying on innovation, and offering customized products.

Born global firms or international new ventures have been considered to be an expression of international entrepreneurship, which has emerged as a new research area at the interface of entrepreneurship and international business (McDougall and Oviatt 2000; Zucchella and Scabini 2007).

Studies of international new ventures suggest a different approach to internationalization from that proposed by stage theorists. Both perspectives build on a knowledge-based view of internationalization. However, the Uppsala model focuses on market knowledge, whereas studies on born global firms emphasize the role of technological knowledge, and their examples of rapidly internationalizing firms are drawn mostly from high-tech industries such as software and biotechnology (Gassmann and Keupp 2007).

The key lesson to be learned from these two research streams is that a firm has to manage its technology-based and marketing resources in accordance with what is required by its foreign development. From a dynamic perspective, as companies go through different stages of internationalization, they need to reconsider their sources of international competitiveness. This highlights the importance of a firm's set of resources and capabilities as drivers of internationalization.

1.2.3 A Resource-Based View of Internationalization

When analyzing the factors affecting the internationalization of SMEs, some studies rely on resource-based literature (Bloodgood et al. 1996; Dhanaraj and Beamish 2003). From a resource-based perspective, firms are collections of unique bundles of resources creating a competitive advantage (Wernerfelt 1984). This set of firm-specific resources and competences forms the basis of the strategic behaviour of a firm, including its internationalization choices, which may be interpreted as how these resources and competences are exploited on a broader scale. Resources are used to create inimitable capabilities (Amit and Schoemaker 1993; Barney 1991).

Resources are the basis of a firm's capabilities, whereas capabilities represent the way it uses its resources. It is not only important to exploit existing capabilities, but also to engage in developing new capabilities (Teece et al. 1997). A capability-based perspective emphasizes a more dynamic view of competition by focusing on a firm's business processes rather than on its assets or resources (Zollo and Winter 2002).

Resource-based-view scholars argue that differences between firms in terms of resources and capabilities explain differential above-average performance within and across industries. Whether they are in developed or emerging economies, in order to survive and grow, firms need to exploit both their existing firm-specific capabilities and develop new ones (Penrose 1959).

SMEs generally lack sophisticated managerial structures. This is particularly relevant in developing countries where firms typically possess less managerial expertise and fewer organizational resources and staff than their counterparts in developed countries (Ibeh 2004).

Building on the resource-based view, a number of studies explain the influence of certain resources on the internationalization of SMEs (Bloodgood et al. 1996; Westhead et al. 2001; Dhanaraj and Beamish 2003). Resources range from physical and tangible, to intangible and knowledge-based. Any production factor or activity may be considered a resource. However, not all resources or competences enable a firm to develop a sustainable competitive advantage. Firms have to identify the specific resources that offer a source of advantage in the specific environment in which they operate.

Intangible resources are strategic for the internationalization process. Greater knowledge of foreign markets, higher market reputation, relational capabilities and management skills needed to handle the greater complexity associated with foreign operations are examples of resources and capabilities that firms need to enhance in order to be successful in foreign markets.

In particular, the characteristics of management assume a central role (Sapienza et al. 2006): managerial competences are fundamental in order to exploit opportunities for development abroad, manage processes and relationships in new contexts, and create routines that facilitate the undertaking of international operations (Westhead et al. 2001). Some of the most valuable and difficult-to-imitate resources of a firm may be its top managers. This is especially true for small firms, where the role of the entrepreneur, and his/her beliefs, attitudes and expectations, is critical (Wiklund et al. 2003).

1.2.4 Internationalization from a Network-Based Perspective

Contributions drawing on network theory have provided new insights into the process of internationalization by highlighting that, in addition to the firm or entrepreneur, network relationships also provide resources and capabilities (Coviello 2006; Elango and Pattnaik 2007; Hadley and Wilson 2003). From a network perspective, internationalization is defined as the process of developing networks of business relationships in other countries (Johanson and Vahlne 1990).

The network contacts of an entrepreneur, which generally derive from prior experience, enable firms to leverage on critical external resources (Chen 2003; Zhou et al. 2007), and are exploited, especially by smaller firms, to mitigate the limitations arising from size or lack of experience (Bell 1995; Zou and Stan 1998). The 'relational capital' – the resources and mutual benefits incorporated in a relationship between two or more parties (Dyer and Singh 1998) – are therefore a key factor driving a firm's international expansion. Such relationships provide access to technological, production or market resources (Johanson and Vahlne

2003). In addition, the members of a network might receive guidance from more experienced partners.

The literature has largely focused on international alliances as a means to fostering internationalization (Murray et al. 1995; Nordberg et al. 1996). However, domestic interfirm relationships also play a role as a vehicle for achieving greater international competitiveness. Local cooperative agreements do matter for an SME's access to global markets. In their survey of 232 Argentine SMEs, Mesquita and Lazzarini (2008) show that through horizontal ties (relationships involving SMEs in the same industry segment or producing complementary products) and vertical ties (relationships involving SMEs specialized in sequential activities of the value chain) SMEs can overcome the constraints deriving from weak infrastructure and poor institutional environment. Inter-organizational collaborative arrangements act as substitutes for the lack of a strong institutional environment and enable firms to start up a number of export-enhancing activities. Through using networks therefore, SMEs gain better access to global markets.

Being affiliated to a business group has been investigated as another network-based resource affecting the exports and performance of firms in emerging economies (Chacar and Vissa 2005; Khanna and Rivkin 2001; Singh 2009). Social relationships have also been studied by researchers; an entrepreneur's social network is a sub-network within the business network (Ruzzier et al. 2006), and is extremely important in obtaining resources (Hoang and Antoncic 2003).

Network-based research contributions highlight the fact that collaborative arrangements or networks can help firms overcome the 'liability of foreignness'. They have extended the traditional stage model of internationalization based on 'learning by doing'. In fact, learning does not take place solely within individual firms, but may also come *from* and be shared *with* partners. In this way, a company's international pattern of expansion can be profoundly influenced by the set of relationships it is capable of developing (see Chap. 2 for an analysis of SME networks).

1.3 Barriers to SME Export: A Classification

Research into exports and SMEs has addressed two main questions: What are the critical factors that affect the export performance of SMEs? What are the barriers to exports by SMEs?

Exporting is generally the first stage of internationalization (Johanson and Vahlne 1977) and is the most common foreign market entry mode among SMEs, given the lower business risk and resource commitment compared to joint ventures and FDIs. However, a number of export barriers constrain the entry and operation of SMEs in foreign markets. Export barriers can be defined as all those attitudinal, structural, operational, and other constraints that hinder a firm's export activity (Leonidou 1995; Suarez-Ortega 2003).

International business studies have identified a variety of barriers and proposed several classifications (e.g. Leonidou 2000; Miesenbock 1988). Katsikeas and

Morgan (1994) identified four groups: external, operational, internal and informational barriers. Zou and Stan (1998) divide export barriers into internal factors (managers' perceptions and attitudes, the firm's characteristics and competences) and external factors (industry and market characteristics). Similarly, Leonidou (2004) moves from the basic distinction between internal barriers associated with organizational resources/capabilities and the company's export strategy, and external barriers related to the home and host environment within which the firm operates. Examples of internal barriers, which can be controlled, to a certain extent, by the firm, are financial constraints, inadequate administrative staff, a lack of managers with international experience and a poor knowledge of foreign languages. External barriers (and therefore less easily controlled) include government restrictions, competition and economic factors such as tariff and non-tariff barriers, or the lack of appropriate national incentives (Campbell 1996).

Small firms are generally considered to be constrained in their international activities owing to their having fewer resources and experience than their larger counterparts. Under the definition of corporate resource constraints, Leonidou (2000) groups four barriers that indicate lack of managerial, human, and financial resources, which block or hinder the firm from initiating or increasing its export activity: unfamiliarity with conducting foreign business, inadequate/untrained export personnel, prohibitive business risks/costs abroad and shortage of working capital to finance overseas operations. Understanding export obstacles has major implications for policy-makers who have to identify those areas where exporters need greater assistance when arranging support services and incentives (Leonidou 2004).

A classification of export barriers is provided in Fig. 1.1.

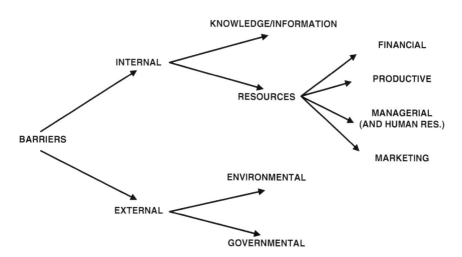

Fig. 1.1 A classification of export barriers (Adapted from Leonidou (2004: 283))

1.3.1 Internal Barriers

Internal barriers can be divided into *knowledge* and *resource* barriers (Ortiz et al. 2008).

Knowledge barriers include:
- *A lack of knowledge of export markets and difficulties associated with the identification of opportunities in foreign countries.* Too little information about the opportunities for a firm's products/services abroad is one of the major barriers. This can be due to either a lack of opportunity to explore new markets or a lack of effort in discovering what opportunities exist (Korth 1991). Information on foreign markets is generally difficult and costly to obtain. Many small firms are not familiar with national and international sources of information. In particular, they often do not have a clear idea about the specific information required in order to identify and analyze potential export markets. Brouthers and Nakos (2005) have shown that the international performance of SMEs is affected by the extent to which they take a systematic approach to selecting export markets: the more systematic the selection, the better the firm's performance.
- *A lack of knowledge of export assistance programmes and public incentives.* Public export incentives should be considered a secondary stimulus as they represent a merely external driver (Christensen et al. 1987). Management decisions should build primarily on a company's awareness of the benefits to be gained from exporting. In many cases SMEs ignore the financial and non-financial benefits associated with exporting (Gripsrud 1990);
- *Language and cultural differences.* These are among the most frequently mentioned barriers in the literature on exporting (Bauerschmidt et al. 1985; Leonidou 2004; Rabino 1980). In contrast to domestic firms, exporters have to face a number of issues associated with differences in culture, behaviour of customers and suppliers, and language and communication. The primary gap a firm needs to fill when going international is that of language, which represents a major gateway to a more profound understanding of the foreign culture.

Resource barriers arise from a lack of resources needed to perform international activities successfully. These include financial, production, marketing, managerial and human resources.
- *Financial resources.* Insufficient financial resources have been identified as a key factor in determining the failure of export ventures. These barriers are associated with both a lack of working capital to finance export sales and a lack of finance for market research, as well as difficulties associated with operating with different currencies and collecting payments abroad (Ortiz et al. 2008).
- *Production resources.* Many SMEs do not have a strategic approach but '*view exporting as a peripheral business activity, undertaken only if there is availability of production resources*' (Leonidou 2004: 288). Insufficient production capacity therefore prevents a firm from devoting some of its production to export markets (Westhead et al. 2002).

- *Marketing resources.* Gaps on the marketing side may be associated with one or more marketing levers. This category includes issues related to a company's product, pricing, distribution, logistics and promotional activities abroad (Kedia and Chhokar 1986; Leonidou 2004; Moini 1997). Export barriers may arise from difficulties in adapting products to the requirements of foreign markets in terms of customer preferences and conditions of use. The main obstacle, especially in the case of firms in developing countries intending to export to more advanced economies, is the difficulty in meeting the quality standards required abroad. Customers in developed countries are generally used to higher quality than that offered by firms in developing countries. Furthermore, developed countries are characterized by stricter regulations, such as those related to customer health and safety. These oblige SMEs in developing countries to make a number of changes to the product which may be excessively costly (Leonidou 2004), or even impossible to achieve, depending upon the firms' internal competences and resources. A lack of adequate after-sales services, difficulties in selecting a reliable distributor, and a limited ability to communicate with foreign customers are other major barriers related to marketing resources (Kaynak et al. 1987).
- *Managerial and human resources.* Management skills and experience are crucial factors for internationalization (Ibeh 2003). Managerial resources and capabilities involve the ability to create, maintain, negotiate and develop appropriate relationships with customers in export markets (Morgan et al. 2004), as well as an ability to obtain important market information. However, SMEs often lack appropriate managerial resources. SME managers tend to focus on decisions relating to everyday questions and may neglect long-term strategic objectives and activities, such as analyzing trends in international markets and developing new capabilities to enter new markets. As a result, SMEs find it more difficult to monitor the international marketplace and assess their strengths and weaknesses. The lack of qualified personnel has been found to be a significant internal resource barrier to exporting (Pinho and Martins 2010; Rabino 1980; Tesfom and Luts 2006; Tseng and Yu 1991). SMEs often experience difficulties in hiring specialized personnel (Ortiz et al. 2008), and this can become a significant constraint to international growth.

1.3.2 External Barriers

External barriers include exogenous, environmental obstacles and uncertainties in international markets that cannot be controlled by firms. These barriers have been variously classified (Moini 1997; Morgan and Katsikeas 1997). Exchange rate fluctuations, poor economic conditions and lack of government support are examples of external barriers to export. In broad terms, we can distinguish environmental and governmental barriers.

Environmental Barriers

Environmental barriers to export may be related both to factors in the home market and conditions in the foreign market where the firm wishes to operate (Leonidou 2004). The economic, political, regulatory and socio-cultural environment of the foreign market the company is planning to operate in may give rise to a number of barriers to export. Poor economic conditions or high competitive pressures greatly reduce business opportunities abroad. Similarly, political instability, risks associated with foreign currency exchange and strict foreign country regulations represent constraints on exporting activities.

Further external barriers which have been identified are: unfamiliarity with foreign business practices and exporting procedures, difficulties in communication with foreign customers and slow collection of payments from abroad (Leonidou 2004).

Governmental Barriers

A number of important constraints on exporting activity also derive from governmental and regulatory issues of both the home and host countries. On the one hand, firms may suffer from a lack of government assistance and incentives for exporting as well as a particularly restrictive regulatory framework concerning export practices; on the other, foreign country regulation may result in a number of restrictions on firms that want to sell their products in that market. Foreign countries may raise tariff or non-tariff barriers in order to create a favourable bias for indigenous firms. However, increasing liberalization is greatly reducing this type of barrier to export.

The lack of support from public agencies may be a relevant barrier to SME export. Support programmes may include a variety of activities, designed to provide either informational or experiential knowledge (Kotabe and Helsen 2008). The former generally comes from 'how-to' export assistance, seminars and workshops while the latter is provided via organization of commercial missions abroad and participation in foreign trade shows. Such support is much more important in developing countries where SMEs are generally characterized by greater constraints in terms of resources and experience, compared to their counterparts in developed countries. In many countries small firms often complain that they receive either insufficient export assistance, or none at all. In addition, it is considered increasingly important for policy-makers to develop their ability to tailor export promotion programmes to the requirements of different exporting groups (Leonidou 2004; Moini 1998).

1.4 Firm Resources, Management Characteristics and SME Exporting Activity

A well-developed body of literature focuses on the effects of a variety of firm-specific and environmental determinants of exporting activity (Cavusgil and Zou 1994; Zou and Stan 1998). The characteristics of a firm and its management, together with environmental factors, affect the export decision-making and performance of SMEs. Aaby and Slater (1989) identified four groups of factors affecting the export behaviour of SMEs: their characteristics (size, managerial commitment and perceptions), competences (such as technology, market knowledge, quality control, communication skills), export strategy (market selection, product mix, product development, promotion, pricing) and the external environment. Zou and Stan (1998) divided these into internal factors (export strategy, managers' perceptions and attitudes, the firm's characteristics and competences) and external factors (industry characteristics and foreign and domestic market factors).

Firm size is one of the most studied factors affecting export. It is considered a proxy for the total resources available to the firm for internationalization processes. Larger firms have more 'slack' managerial, productive and financial resources, and can therefore meet the challenges of internationalization more easily. Many researchers have assumed that larger firms tend to be better international performers. However, this view is not universally supported by empirical evidence. Studies of the relationship between firm size and internationalization highlight the fact that being small does not per se constitute an export barrier and that, despite their fewer resources, SMEs can successfully enter foreign markets and reach high export levels (Bonaccorsi 1992; Calof 1993). Calof's analysis of small and medium-sized Canadian firms showed that a firm's size limits only the number of markets served. In his study of a large sample of Italian exporting firms, Bonaccorsi (1992) found that size correlated positively with the propensity to export, and correlated negatively with export intensity (the ratio between export and total sales). In general, the literature on size-export relationships has produced mixed results. Similarly, analyses of the effect of the age of a firm and its export performance have led to controversial results.

Innovation can also have a significant positive influence on export. Technology is one of the key resources of a firm. In their study of the resource-based approach to export performance, Dhanaraj and Beamish (2003) found that technological intensity is a good predictor of export strategy which, in turn, has a positive effect on a firm's performance. Firms with lower levels of technology tend to focus on domestic or less demanding foreign markets.

Compared to domestic firms, international firms have to face additional issues due to differences in terms of culture, ethical standards and language. Export (or any other international activity) makes it necessary for SMEs to have a greater set of capabilities and competences than purely domestic SMEs. Human capital, in particular, is considered significant in explaining the internationalization of SMEs. In small firms, constraints in terms of human resources make the task of identifying and operating in foreign markets more problematic (Gomez-Mejia 1988).

Human capital may be defined as consisting of education, experience and skills (Boxall and Steeneveld 1999; Rauch et al. 2005). In a broad sense, it is related to the training, qualifications, experience and technical abilities of personnel (Ashton and Green 1996). A certain qualification does not automatically imply the possession of the necessary skill to work in a particular industry, nor do skilled workers necessarily have a specific qualification (Devins 2008). However, a higher level of education is associated with greater knowledge, useful for the management of complex decision-making processes as well as for the analysis of the international environment. Apart from the technical competences acquired, a higher level of education can create the opportunity to encounter new contexts and people, and tends therefore to favour a greater propensity for change (Tihanyi et al. 2000; Wiersema and Bantel 1992). These factors are important in managing the challenges of international development and understanding different ways of doing business.

Research has also explored the relationships between a number of characteristics of decision-makers and SME export performance (Cavusgil and Zou 1994; Contractor et al. 2005; Mittelstaedt et al. 2003; Reid 1983). The age and education level of decision-makers have been analyzed as predictors of international success, although empirical evidence does not seem to show a clear relationship (Manolova et al. 2002). Research has also indicated that managers' motivations and attitudes to growth can affect a firm's international activities. Leonidou et al. (1998) divided the characteristics of management which affect export into four categories: general-objective (age group, educational background, professional experience); specific-objective (ethnic origin, language proficiency, time spent abroad, foreign travel); general-subjective (risk tolerance, innovativeness, flexibility, commitment, dynamism) and specific-subjective (perceptions of risk, costs, profits, growth and complexity).

Decision-makers play a crucial role in export activities, especially in the case of SMEs whose limited size means that the entrepreneur him/herself is often in charge of export activities, and that there is a considerable overlap between him/her and the organization. Strategic decisions in SMEs are typically made by one person, often the owner-manager. Therefore, when the SME is developing in an international market, the role of the entrepreneur in defining strategies and orientating growth paths is still of great importance (Knight 2001; Lamb and Liesch 2002). However, it emerges that the need for organizational development and new roles within the firm is even greater. Beyond the entrepreneur and the management team, other individuals play an important role in the success and growth of SMEs.

With an increasing commitment in foreign markets, the number of people within the firm involved in managing international activities also increases (e.g. contact with clients and suppliers and management of commercial and productive subsidiaries). Consequently, the need to access qualified personnel with the necessary competences to manage a process of international growth successfully becomes imperative. The pursuance of international development strategies by SMEs therefore brings the role of employees' human capital into the foreground.

Employees' knowledge and skills are valuable resources. Human resources are more critical to the achievement of competitive advantage than tangible or financial resources, as they are more likely to possess those characteristics (e.g. valuable, difficult to imitate or substitute) which scholars of the resource-based view have identified as sources of competitive advantage (Barney 1991). Human capital is considered to be crucial to the recognition and exploitation of business opportunities. Therefore, as well as financial issues, human capital is also of critical importance as a resource for internationalization, as recent empirical evidence shows (Cerrato and Piva 2012).

Methodological problems affect the findings of studies on factors affecting SMEs' exports (Singh 2009).

Firstly, we cannot ignore the interdependence of export sales and domestic sales. Export sales have been analyzed in isolation, although it is reasonable to assume that export and domestic sales are simultaneously determined (Salomon and Shaver 2005). A strategic management perspective highlights the different strategic options for a firm, in terms of market segments and products. On the other hand, an international business perspective tends to neglect domestic or product-market strategic choices (Karafyllia 2009). As a result, the inter-relationships between domestic and international markets, which are particularly important for smaller firms, have received limited attention (Singh 2009).

Secondly, most studies have been conducted on firms in developed economies. The peculiar business environment of developing and emerging countries calls into question the generalizability of the findings of studies based on data from advanced economies. It is reasonable to assume that country differences affect the patterns of SMEs' foreign expansion. Such differences must therefore be taken into account in the analysis of SME internationalization.

1.5 The Characteristics of Developing Countries

Countries are generally classified according to their level of development. Such classifications are often misleading as conditions in countries change over time.

The traditional developed/developing country dichotomy became the most common way to classify countries in the 1960s. Over time, this was increasingly considered to be too restrictive and new classifications with more than two categories were introduced to better capture differences across countries. Country taxonomies have been developed by the United Nations, the World Bank, and the International Monetary Fund (IMF). They are similar in terms of identifying a country as developed or developing. However, there is no generally agreed classification criterion. The approaches behind the construction of these taxonomies are different, due to the different mandates of these institutions (Nielsen 2011). In addition, the concept of development itself is difficult to define.

In general, given the high levels of heterogeneity within the group of developing countries, taxonomies identify different subgroups. Specifically, the *IMF* distinguishes between 'low-income developing countries' and 'emerging and other developing countries'. The United Nations Development Program identifies low, medium and high human development countries, whereas the World Bank classifies developing countries as either low-income or middle-income countries.

In broad terms, by developing countries we mean low-income countries still characterized by limited industrialization and stagnant economies (Cavusgil et al. 2008). They include low-income countries in Africa, Latin America and Asia.

Consumers in developing countries have a very low discretionary income. The proportion of personal income spent on goods other than food, clothing and housing is very limited. Governments in developing countries are often heavily indebted and bureaucracy greatly constrains the chances for the survival and growth of small firms.

The economic growth of developing countries relies on a greater engagement of these countries in international trade. Participating actively in international trade can significantly stimulate economic growth and stability in developing countries and help create jobs and raise income. Promoting a higher level of exports can therefore be crucial for governments and policy-makers in order to make countries more successful in terms of development.

Emerging market economies represent a subset of former developing economies that have achieved substantial industrialization, improved living standards, and remarkable economic growth. 'Emerging markets' and 'transition economies' are partially overlapping concepts. The difference lies in the starting point for the transition to a market economy (Jansson 2009). Transition economies refer to the countries of the former Soviet bloc in Eastern Europe and Central Asia plus China, Vietnam and Mongolia in East Asia, which are undergoing a transformation from a centrally-planned to a market economy. In the other emerging markets, on the other hand, there was no communist regime.

The terms 'emerging' and 'transition' imply that some form of change is underway, in terms of transformation of the key aspects of the economy (Johnson and Turner 2010). In general, they are experiencing change from developing to developed country status. To various extents, these countries are introducing economic reform in the direction of greater market freedom. Reducing restrictions on business activities, privatization, development of market institutions and more efficient financial systems, lower trade barriers and greater acceptance of inward investors are all milestones in such a change.

Hoskisson et al. (2000) identified emerging economies with countries that have gained increasing importance over the years due to their large populations, rapid economic development and increased contribution to world trade. Despite the differences between them, these included 51 high-growth developing economies in Latin America, Asia, Africa and the Middle East, and 13 transition economies in the former Soviet Union. Countries such as Brazil, Argentina, Mexico, India, China, Pakistan and South Africa are examples of emerging markets.

Emerging countries and transition economies are characterized by rapid economic growth and institutional changes towards liberalization and market-based mechanisms of organizing economic activities (Hoskisson et al. 2000; Peng 2003; Wright et al. 2005).

Firms from developing and emerging countries are characterized by a number of resource disadvantages compared to firms from advanced economies (Singh 2009). To differing extents these countries are experiencing a relaxation of constraints on entrepreneurial activities resulting in the exploitation of greater entrepreneurial opportunities by local firms as well as the exploration of new market opportunities through export activities.

Enhancing the competitiveness of SMEs is crucial to the generation of employment opportunities and to the growth of developing countries. This objective is at the root of a number of governmental and non-governmental programmes which aim to contribute to a significant reduction in constraints on greater firm competitiveness.

1.6 Patterns of SME International Expansion

Internationalization has traditionally been analyzed within the context of mature developed economies, but today's economic environment is characterized by the increasing importance of emerging economies. This change raises questions as to whether, and to what extent, the conventional theories and models are suitable for explaining the patterns of international expansion of firms from such economies (Wright et al. 2005).

In comparison with those in developed countries, firms in emerging/developing economies have fewer managerial resources and fewer private or public support services, both of which negatively affect their ability to go international. However, their role in international trade is dramatically increasing, and empirical evidence shows that their internationalization pathways may be more heterogeneous than those assumed by traditional models such as the stage theory (see Sect. 1.2.1).

The internationalization of a firm has been commonly considered to be a process driven by learning about foreign markets: as a firm acquires greater experience and knowledge of foreign markets, it can develop its ability to market its products abroad and serve foreign customers as successfully as its domestic customers (Johanson and Wiedersheim-Paul 1975; Johanson and Vahlne 1977). Involvement in internationalization has been conceptualized as a result of greater competences and capabilities in marketing, selling and customer-servicing activities, and a greater knowledge of international trends and customer preferences. It has therefore been analyzed in relation to downstream activities, especially marketing. The conventional model of internationalization in developed countries focuses on the marketing of goods and services in foreign countries through exports (Kuada and Sorensen 2000).

However, globalization has profoundly changed the organization of international production with important implications for developing countries (Johnson and Turner 2010). Increasing economic integration has enhanced the emergence of global manufacturing systems in which different production processes are dispersed on a global basis. This has shown the relevance of a different route to international markets. In developing countries, an increasing number of firms go international by becoming contract manufacturers in a global value chain, created and coordinated by an MNE.

The literature on the global value chain (Gereffi 1999; Humphrey and Schmitz 2002) highlights the opportunities for local SMEs to upgrade their business processes through integration within global value chains. This research shows that MNEs which act as leaders of the value chain on a global basis play a key role in

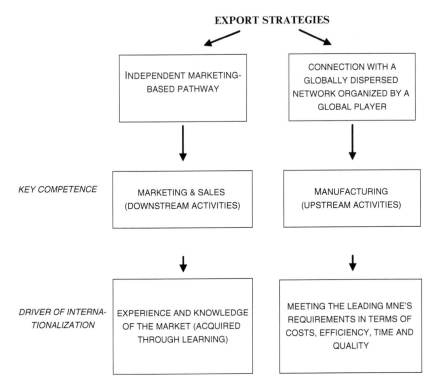

Fig. 1.2 Patterns of foreign expansion

providing opportunities for small local producers, in terms of learning and promotion of process, product and functional upgrading (Giuliani et al. 2005; Humphrey 1995; Humphrey and Schmitz 2002).

The two pathways are characterized by a number of differences (Fig. 1.2). We define the first as the *independent marketing-based pathway*: an independent firm gradually gains experience and knowledge of foreign markets and, by doing so, strengthens its ability to meet the needs of foreign customers and serve them as efficiently as it serves its domestic customers.

In the second model, knowledge of foreign customers is not the key driver of internationalization. Serving customers abroad is not crucial, because an MNE provides entry to foreign markets for the SMEs included in its global value chain. This pathway can be defined as an *export strategy based on incorporation in an MNE's global value chain* (Gereffi 1999; Humphrey and Schmitz 2002). In this case, which is typical of firms in emerging markets, the key task is not so much the acquisition of greater market knowledge, but the development of a sustainable competitive advantage, particularly in manufacturing. The focus here is on upstream activity. Competitive advantages associated with marketing and customer relationships belong to the global player coordinating its value chain on a global basis. Relationships with distributors and end-users, as well as customer services, are controlled by the leading MNE from a developed country (Schmitz and Knorringa 2000). The internationalization of SMEs in this case is based on a production contract with a leading firm: SMEs would not be able to handle the whole export process on their own as they lack the required competences and capabilities.

Moreover, it is important to point out that international activities do not necessarily start with exports. Many SMEs start going international on the inward rather than the outward side, and importing activities may subsequently have positive effects on exports (Depperu 1993). Firms can acquire international experience by means of imports related to their production (Kuada and Sorensen 2000), and this experience may be useful for subsequent export activity.

In conclusion, firms, especially those from emerging and developing markets, may follow different successful pathways depending on whether their international competitiveness is developed in relation to upstream or downstream activities – or both. Some firms achieve export success mainly through international competitiveness in upstream activities, particularly manufacturing; others develop core competences in downstream activities, such as marketing and sales. Hybrid models may arise from combining the two: for example, when a firm has a dominant customer, but is simultaneously able to sell its products to end-users directly.

Following a 'contingency' approach, it may be argued that a company's international development is contingent upon a wide range of industry-, country- and firm-specific factors (Robertson and Chetty 2000). The different internationalization pathways of a firm also have different implications for policy-makers. The two models are characterized by different export barriers and requirements in terms of resources and competences, and these must be taken into account by governments interested in setting up incentives and support services.

References

Aaby, N. E., & Slater, S. (1989). Management influences on export performance: A review of the empirical literature 1978–88. *International Marketing Review, 6*(4), 7–25.

Amit, R., & Schoemaker, P. (1993). Strategic assets and organizational rent. *Strategic Management Journal, 14*(1), 33–46.

Andersson, S. (2004). Internationalization in different industrial contexts. *Journal of Business Venturing, 19*(6), 851–875.

Ashton, D., & Green, F. (1996). *Education, training and the global economy.* Aldershot: Elgar.

Barney, J. B. (1991). Firm resources and sustained competitive advantage. *Journal of Management, 17*(1), 99–120.

Bauerschmidt, A., Sullivan, D., & Gillespie, K. (1985). Common factors underlying barriers to export: A comparative study in the US paper industry. *Journal of International Business Studies, 16*(3), 111–123.

Bell, J. (1995). The internationalization of small computer software firms: A further challenge to stage theories. *European Journal of Marketing, 29*(8), 60–75.

Bell, J., McNaughton, R. B., Young, S., & Crick, D. (2003). Towards an integrative model of small firm internationalisation. *Journal of International Entrepreneurship, 1*(4), 339–62.

Bloodgood, J. M., Sapienza, H. J., & Almeida, J. G. (1996). The internationalization of new high potential U.S. ventures: Antecedents and outcomes. *Entrepreneurship Theory and Practice, 20*(4), 61–76.

Bonaccorsi, A. (1992). On the relationship between firm size and export intensity. *Journal of International Business Studies, 23*(4), 605–635.

Boxall, P., & Steeneveld, M. (1999). Human resource strategy and competitive advantage: A longitudinal study of engineering consultancies. *Journal of Management Studies, 36*(4), 443–463.

Brouthers, L. E., & Nakos, G. (2005). The role of systematic international market selection on small firms' export performance. *Journal of Small Business Management, 43*(4), 363–81.

Buckley, P., & Casson, M. (1976). *The future of the multinational enterprise*. New York: Holmes & Meier.

Calof, J. L. (1993). The impact of size on internationalization. *Journal of Small Business Management, 31*(4), 60–69.

Campbell, A. J. (1996). The effects of internal firm barriers on the export behavior of small firms in a free trade environment. *Journal of Small Business Management, 34*(3), 50–58.

Cavusgil, S. T., & Zou, S. (1994). Marketing strategy-performance relationship: An investigation of the empirical link in export market ventures. *Journal of Marketing, 58*(1), 1–21.

Cavusgil, S. T., Knight, G., & Riesenberger, J. R. (2008). *International business. Strategy, management, and the new realities*. Upper Saddle River: Pearson Prentice Hall.

Cerrato, D., & Piva, M. (2012). The internationalization of small and medium-sized enterprises: The effect of family management, human capital and foreign ownership. *Journal of Management and Governance*, forthcoming.

Chacar, A., & Vissa, B. (2005). Are emerging economies less efficient? Performance persistence and the impact of business group affiliation. *Strategic Management Journal, 26*(10), 933–946.

Chen, T. J. (2003). Network resources for internationalization: The case of Taiwan's electronics firms. *Journal of Management Studies, 40*(5), 1107–1130.

Christensen, C. H., Da Rocha, A., & Gertner, R. (1987). An empirical investigation of the factors influencing export success of Brazilian firms. *Journal of International Business Studies, 18*(3), 61–77.

Contractor, J. J., Hsu, C.-C., & Kundu, S. K. (2005). Explaining export performance: A comparative study of international new ventures in Indian and Taiwanese software industry. *Management International Review, 45*(3), 83–110.

Coviello, N. E. (2006). The network dynamics of international new ventures. *Journal of International Business Studies, 37*(5), 713–731.

Depperu, D. (1993). *L'internazionalizzazione delle piccole e medie imprese*. Milano: Egea.

Devins, D. (2008). Encouraging skills acquisitions and SMEs. In R. Barret & S. Mayson (Eds.), *International handbook of entrepreneurship and HRM* (pp. 420–433). Cheltenham: Elgar.

Dhanaraj, C., & Beamish, P. W. (2003). A resource-based approach to the study of export performance. *Journal of Small Business Management, 41*(3), 242–261.

Dunning, J. H. (1981). *International production and the multinational enterprise*. London: Allen & Unwin.

Dyer, J. H., & Singh, H. (1998). The relational view: Cooperative strategy and sources of interorganizational competitive advantage. *Academy of Management Review, 23*(4), 660–679.

Elango, B., & Pattnaik, C. (2007). Building capabilities for international operations through networks: A study of Indian firms. *Journal of International Business Studies, 38*(4), 541–555.

Gassmann, O. & Keupp, M. M. (2007). The competitive advantage of early and rapidly internationalising SMEs in the biotechnology industry: A knowledge-based view. *Journal of World Business, 42*(3), 350–366

Gereffi, G. (1999). International trade and industrial upgrading in the apparel commodity chain. *Journal of International Economics, 48*(1), 37–70.

Giuliani, E., Pietrobelli, C., & Rabellotti, R. (2005). Upgrading in global value chains: Lessons from Latin American clusters. *World Development, 33*(4), 549–573.

References

Gomez-Mejia, L. R. (1988). The role of human resources strategy in export performance: A longitudinal study. *Strategic Management Journal, 9*(5), 493–505.

Gripsrud, G. (1990). The determinants of export decisions and attitudes to a distant market: Norwegian fishery exports to Japan. *Journal of International Business Studies, 21*(3), 469–485.

Hadley, R. D., & Wilson, H. I. M. (2003). The network model of internationalisation and experiential knowledge. *International Business Review, 12*(6), 697–717.

Hoang, H., & Antoncic, B. (2003). Network based research in entrepreneurship: A critical review. *Journal of Business Venturing, 18*(2), 165–187.

Hoskisson, R. E., Eden, L., Lau, C.-M., & Wright, M. (2000). Strategy in emerging economies. *Academy of Management Journal, 43*(3), 249–267.

Humphrey, J. (Ed.) (1995). Industrial organization and manufacturing competitiveness in developing countries. *World Development*, Special Issue, *23*(1), 1–7.

Humphrey, J., & Schmitz, H. (2002). How does insertion in global value chains affect upgrading industrial clusters? *Regional Studies, 36*(9), 1017–1027.

Hymer, S. H. (1976). *The international operations of foreign firms: A study of direct foreign investment*. Cambridge: MIT (originally, Ph.D. dissertation, MIT, 1960).

Ibeh, K. I. N. (2003). Toward a contingency framework of export entrepreneurship: Conceptualisations and empirical evidence. *Small Business Economics, 15*(1), 49–68.

Ibeh, K. I. N. (2004). Furthering export participation in less performing developing countries: The effects of entrepreneurial orientation and managerial capacity factors. *International Journal of Social Economics, 31*(1/2), 94–110.

Jansson, H. (2009). *International business marketing in emerging country markets. The third wave of internationalization of firms*. Cheltenham: Edward Elgar.

Johanson, J., & Vahlne, J. E. (1977). The internationalization process of the firm: A model of knowledge development and increasing foreign market commitments. *Journal of International Business Studies, 8*(1), 23–32.

Johanson, J., & Vahlne, J.-E. (1990). The mechanism of internationalization. *International Marketing Review, 7*(4), 11–24.

Johanson, J., & Vahlne, J. E. (2003). Business relationship learning and commitment in the internationalization process. *Journal of International Entrepreneurship, 1*(1), 83–101.

Johanson, J., & Wiedersheim-Paul, F. (1975). The internationalization of the firm: Four Swedish cases. *Journal of Management Studies, 12*(3), 305–322.

Johnson, D., & Turner, C. (2010). *International business. Themes and issues in the modern global economy* (2nd ed.). London: Routledge.

Karafyllia, M. (2009). Perspectives on the interrelationships between domestic and international markets for the smaller firm. In M. V. Jones, P. Dimitratos, M. Flecther, & S. Young (Eds.), *Internationalization, entrepreneurship and the smaller firm* (pp. 53–72). Cheltenham: Edward Elgar.

Katsikeas, C., & Morgan, R. E. (1994). Differences in perceptions of exporting problems based on firm size and export market experience. *European Journal of Marketing, 28*(5), 17–35.

Kaynak, E., Ghauri, P. N., & Olofsson-Bredenlöw, T. (1987). Export behavior of small Swedish firms. *Journal of Small Business Management, 25*(2), 26–32.

Kedia, B. L., & Chhokar, J. (1986). Factors inhibiting export performance of firms: An empirical investigation. *Management International Review, 26*(4), 33–43.

Khanna, T., & Rivkin, J. W. (2001). Estimating the performance effects of business groups in emerging markets. *Strategic Management Journal, 22*(1), 45–74.

Knight, G. A. (2001). Entrepreneurship and strategy in the international SME. *Journal of International Management, 7*(3), 155–171.

Knight, G., & Cavusgil, S. T. (1996). The born global firm: A challenge to traditional internationalization theory. In S. T. Cavusgil & T. Madsen (Eds.), *Advances in international marketing* (Vol. 8, pp. 11–26). Greenwich: JAI Press.

Korth, C.M. (1991). Managerial barriers to export. *Business horizons* (pp. 18–26), March-April.

Kotabe, M., & Helsen, K. (2008). *Global marketing management* (4th ed.). Hoboken: John Wiley & Sons.

Kuada, J., & Sorensen, O. J. (2000). *Internationalization of companies from developing countries*. New York: International Business Press.

Lamb, P. W., & Liesch, P. W. (2002). The internationalization process of smaller firms: Reframing the relationships between market commitment, knowledge and involvement. *Management International Review, 42*(1), 7–26.

Leonidou, L. C. (1995). Empirical research on export barriers: Review, assessment, and synthesis. *Journal of International Management, 3*(1), 29–43.

Leonidou, L. C. (2000). Barriers to export management: An organizational and internationalization analysis. *Journal of International Management, 6*(2), 121–148.

Leonidou, L. C. (2004). An analysis of the barriers hindering small business export development. *Journal of Small Business Management, 42*(3), 279–302.

Leonidou, L., & Katsikeas, C. (1996). The export development process: An integrative review of empirical models. *Journal of International Business Studies, 27*(3), 517–551.

Leonidou, L. C., Katsikeas, C. S., & Piercy, N. F. (1998). Identifying managerial influences on exporting: Past research and future directions. *Journal of International Marketing, 6*(2), 74–102.

Madsen, T. K., & Servais, P. (1997). The internationalization of born globals – an evolutionary process? *International Business Review, 6*(6), 561–583.

Manolova, T., Brush, C., Edelman, L., & Greene, P. (2002). Internationalization of small firms: Personal factors revisited. *International Small Business Journal, 20*(1), 9–30.

McDougall, P. P., & Oviatt, B. M. (2000). International entrepreneurship: The intersection of two research paths. *Academy of Management Journal, 43*(5), 902–906.

McDougall, P. P., Shane, S., & Oviatt, B. M. (1994). Explaining the formation of international new ventures. *Journal of Business Venturing, 9*(6), 469–487.

Mesquita, L. F., & Lazzarini, S. G. (2008). Horizontal and vertical relationships in developing economies: Implications for SMEs' access to global markets. *Academy of Management Journal, 51*(2), 359–380.

Miesenbock, K. J. (1988). Small business and exporting: A literature review. *International Small Business Journal, 6*(2), 42–61.

Mittelstaedt, J. D., Harben, G. N., & Ward, W. A. (2003). How small is too small? Firm size as a barrier to exporting from the United States. *Journal of Small Business Management, 41*(1), 68–84.

Moini, A. H. (1997). Barriers inhibiting export performance of small and medium-sized manufacturing firms. *Journal of Global Marketing, 10*(4), 67–93.

Moini, A. H. (1998). Small firms exporting: how effective are government export assistance programs? *Journal of Small Business Management, 36*(1), 1–15.

Morgan, R. E., & Katsikeas, C. S. (1997). Export stimuli: Export intention compared with export activity. *International Business Review, 6*(5), 477–499.

Morgan, R. E., Kaleka, A., & Katsikeas, C. S. (2004). Antecedents of export venture performance: A theoretical model and empirical assessment. *Journal of Marketing, 68*(1), 90–108.

Murray, J. Y., Masaaki, K., & Wildt, A. R. (1995). Strategic and financial performance implications of global sourcing strategy: A contingency analysis. *Journal of International Business Studies, 26*(1), 181–202.

Nielsen (2011). *Classifications of countries based on their level of development: How it is done and how it could be done*, IMF Working Paper.

Nordberg, M., Campbell, A. J., & Verbeke, A. (1996). Can market based contracts substitute for alliances in high technology markets? *Journal of International Business Studies, 27*(5), 963–979.

Ortiz, J. A., Ortiz, R. F., & Ramírez, A. M. (2008). *An integrative classification of barriers to exporting: An empirical analysis in small and medium-sized enterprises*. Paper presented at the 50th AIB conference, 30 June–3 July, Milan.

References

Oviatt, B. M., & McDougall, P. P. (1994). Toward a theory of international new ventures. *Journal of International Business Studies, 25*(1), 45–64.

Oviatt, B. M., & McDougall, P. P. (1995). Global start-ups: Entrepreneurs on a worldwide stage. *Academy of Management Executive, 9*(2), 30–44.

Peng, M. W. (2003). Institutional transitions and strategic choices. *Academy of Management Review, 28*(2), 275–296.

Penrose, E. (1959). *The theory of growth of the firm.* Oxford: Blackwell.

Pinho, J. C., & Martins, L. (2010). Exporting barriers: Insights from Portuguese small- and medium-sized exporters and non-exporters. *Journal of international Entrepreneurship, 8*(3), 254–272.

Rabino, S. (1980). An examination of barriers to exporting encountered by small manufacturing companies. *Management International Review, 20*(1), 67–73.

Ramaseshan, B., & Soutar, G. N. (1996). Combined effects of incentives and barriers on firms' export decisions. *International Business Review, 5*(1), 53–65.

Rauch, A., Frese, M., & Utsch, A. (2005). Effects of human capital and long-term human resources development and utilization on employment growth of small-scale businesses: A causal analysis. *Entrepreneurship Theory and Practice, 29*(6), 681–698.

Reid, S. (1983). Managerial and firm influences on export behaviour. *Journal of the Academy of Marketing Science, 11*(3), 323–332.

Robertson, C., & Chetty, S. (2000). A contingency-based approach to understanding export performance. *International Business Review, 9*(2), 211–35.

Ruzzier, M., Hisrich, R. D., & Antoncic, B. (2006). SME internationalization research: Past, present, and future. *Journal of Small Business and Enterprise Development, 13*(4), 476–497.

Salomon, R., & Shaver, J. M. (2005). Export and domestic sales: Their interrelationship and determinants. *Strategic Management Journal, 26*(9), 855–871.

Sapienza, H. J., Autio, E., George, G., & Zahra, S. A. (2006). A capabilities perspective on the effects of early internationalization on firm survival and growth. *Academy of Management Review, 31*(4), 914–933.

Schmitz, H. (1995). Collective efficiency: Growth path for small-scale industry. *Journal of Development Studies, 31*(4), 529–567.

Schmitz, H., & Knorringa, P. (2000). Learning from global buyers. *Journal of Development Studies, 37*(2), 177–205.

Singh, D. A. (2009). Export performance of emerging market firms. *International Business Review, 18*(4), 321–330.

Suarez-Ortega, S. (2003). Export barriers: Insights from small and medium-sized firms. *International Small Business Journal, 21*(4), 403–419.

Tallman, S., Jenkins, M., Henry, N., & Pinch, S. (2004). Knowledge, clusters, and competitive advantage. *Academy of Management Review, 29*(2), 258–271.

Teece, D. J., Pisano, G., & Shuen, A. (1997). Dynamic capabilities and strategic management. *Strategic Management Journal, 18*(7), 509–533.

Tesfom, G., & Luts, C. (2006). A classification of export marketing problems of small and medium sized manufacturing firms in developing countries. *International Journal of Emerging Markets, 1*(3), 262–281.

Tihanyi, L., Ellstrand, A. E., Daily, C. M., & Dalton, D. R. (2000). Composition of the top management team and firm international diversification. *Journal of Management, 26*(6), 1157–1177.

Tseng, J., & Yu, C.-M. J. (1991). Export of industrial goods to Europe: The case of large Taiwanese firms. *European Journal of Marketing, 25*(9), 51–63.

Wernerfelt, B. (1984). A resource-based view of the firm. *Strategic Management Journal, 5*(2), 171–80.

Westhead, P., Wright, M., & Ucbasaran, D. (2001). The internationalization of new and small firms: A resource-based view. *Journal of Business Venturing, 16*(4), 333–358.

Westhead, P., Wright, M., & Ucbasaran, D. (2002). International market selection strategies selected by 'micro' and 'small' firms. *Omega, International Journal of Management Science, 30*(1), 51–68.

Wiersema, M. F., & Bantel, K. A. (1992). Top management team demography and corporate strategic change. *Academy of Management Journal, 35*(1), 91–121.

Wiklund, J., Davidsson, P., & Delmar, F. (2003). What do they think and feel about growth? An expectancy-value approach to small business managers' attitudes toward growth. *Entrepreneurship Theory and Practice, 27*(3), 247–270.

Wright, M., Filatotchev, I., Hoskisson, R. E., & Peng, M. W. (2005). Strategy research in emerging economies: Challenging the conventional wisdom. *Journal of Management Studies, 42*(1), 1–33.

Zaheer, S. (1995). Overcoming the liability of foreignness. *Academy of Management Journal, 38*(2), 341–363.

Zhou, L., Wu, W., & Luo, X. (2007). Internationalization and the performance of born-global SMEs: The mediating role of social networks. *Journal of International Business Studies, 38*(4), 673–690.

Zollo, M., & Winter, S. G. (2002). Deliberate learning and the evolution of dynamic capabilities. *Organization Science, 13*(3), 339–351.

Zou, S., & Stan, S. (1998). The determinants of export performance: A review of the empirical literature between 1987 and 1997. *International Marketing Review, 15*(5), 333–356.

Zucchella, A., & Scabini, P. (2007). *International entrepreneurship. Theoretical foundations and practices.* New York: Palgrave Macmillan.

Strategic Networks, Trust and the Competitive Advantage of SMEs

2.1 SME Attitude Towards Cooperation

Since their origins, the studies on entrepreneurship and small business management have often focused on either the personality traits of entrepreneurs or the neoclassical view of micro-economics, assuming the individual firm as an exclusive unit of analysis. More specifically, following the mainstream of the discipline, most strategic management scholars have long analyzed the entrepreneur's behaviour as that of a rational and resourceful individualist, conducting his or her own business according to a stand-alone strategy within a hostile, competitive environment.

Starting from the mid-1980s research has highlighted the relevance of social networks and collaborative strategies as tools for contributing to the development and success of firms, particularly SMEs. Joining a strategic network or alliance has been acknowledged as a valuable path for SMEs striving to gain a sustainable competitive advantage within their business environments: lower transaction costs, social capital creation, entering foreign markets and achieving economies of scale have all been reported as positive outcomes of establishing ties with other firms in the markets (Cruickshank and Rolland 2006; Doz and Hamel 1998; Inkpen and Tsang 2005; Jarillo 1988; Nahapiet and Ghoshal 1998; Rosenfeld 1996). Building on this new social network perspective, the entrepreneurship literature has emphasized the importance of networks to small firms, particularly as a means of obtaining resources which would otherwise be unavailable to them (Aldrich and Zimmer 1986; Starr and MacMillan 1990). In particular, research into entrepreneurship in transition economies shows that social capital is an important determinant of resource acquisition and that many of the competitive advantages of transition economies are based on network relationships (Hoskisson et al. 2000; Manev et al. 2005; Manolova et al. 2002).

The concept of 'network' and 'networking' applied to the strategic management of SMEs helps us focus on entrepreneurship as a collective, rather than an individualistic phenomenon (Johannisson 1987, 2000) and permits the addition of some interesting new options regarding the ways small businesses may build their competitive advantage, in both domestic and international markets. By developing networks, small firms can obtain support for their activities in the domestic market. Moreover, cooperation among SMEs has also proved to be beneficial for promoting exports by favouring both the start-up of export activities and improving export performance. Network-based research has shown that the internationalization process of firms is largely driven by network relationships, the establishment of which is even more important for SMEs, as they face a variety of internal constraints due mainly to the lack of financial and managerial resources.

As discussed in Chap. 1, the international activities of small firms are hindered by their limited resources and capabilities, and the fact that they cannot access comprehensive market research. Furthermore, in most cases, it is not feasible for them to hire experts who can assist them in their internationalization efforts. This is particularly true of SMEs in developing countries, where relatively few entrepreneurs have international experience or a high level of management education. In order to go international, they must not only overcome their own lack of managerial expertise and knowledge of international markets, but also the limited support they can expect from local governments.

A number of studies (Chetty and Agndal 2007; Coviello and Munro 1995, 1997) have shown that SMEs rely extensively on networks in pursuing international opportunities. Network resources also help SMEs to overcome the risks and challenges associated with foreign market entry decisions.

According to Mesquita and Lazzarini (2008), in developing countries – or at least in countries without a supportive environment, due to the weakness of infrastructures and institutions – SMEs can achieve greater efficiencies and obtain access to global markets by building vertical and horizontal ties with other small firms. They support this statement with the results of an empirical analysis of 232 Argentine furniture SMEs in the Province of Buenos Aires, concluding that horizontal relations promote collective sourcing of resources and joint product innovations, while vertical relations can increase manufacturing productivity.

In this book we concentrate specifically on the role of one particular form of domestic interfirm networking among SMEs, that is *export consortia*. This kind of network is presented and discussed in detail in Chapter 3. First, however, in this chapter we introduce the main concepts related to interfirm networks in order to better understand the organizational features and the particular strategic issues related to building a network of SMEs.

2.2 Defining Strategic Networks of SMEs

Since the 1960s, the network metaphor has been employed extensively to analyze any kind of interaction among individuals, groups and organizations. It has, therefore, been applied in many different fields, such as sociology, political science, organization theory and – more recently – business strategy.

2.2 Defining Strategic Networks of SMEs

Nowadays, in a broad sense, we use the term *network* to indicate a social structure that includes a set of relationships between a group of individuals, while the term *networking* is used for the activity by which this kind of structure is built, developed and run.

The concept of network includes four key components: *actors*, *links*, *flows* and *mechanisms* (Conway et al. 2001; Conway and Jones 2006). The *actors* are the individuals that make up the network and are usually represented graphically as the nodes of a web. They may be different kinds of entities, according to the nature of the phenomenon to be analyzed: human beings, places, computers, organizations or – in the case of our area of interest – firms. The *links* (or ties) are the arches that connect individuals/nodes and represent the relationships between the actors. They may have different forms, directions, lengths and intensities. The *flows* indicate the exchanges that occur between the actors within the network and may have different natures and transaction contents: flows of information, advice, money, goods (raw materials, components, and equipment), power, friendship, etc. Finally, the *mechanisms* of the network are the modes and rules of interaction employed by the actors within the networks. Depending on the different aims of the networks, they include face-to-face interactions, meetings, planning, joint participation (for instance) in trade fairs or business seminars and can be more or less structured, formalized, planned and active.

The application of the concept of network (and the subsequent social network approach) to the relationships between business organizations originates in the mid-1980s.

In his seminal work, Thorelli (1986) defines networks as an intermediate form between 'hierarchy' and 'market', the two alternative modes of organizing economic activities described by Williamson (1975). Thorelli sustains that, through building lasting relations with other actors, firms within networks can compete efficiently, reducing the costs of transactions (typical of markets) without incurring large investments (typical of the hierarchical mode of organizing economic activities).

Jarillo (1988) defines *strategic networks* as long-term agreements between different but linked organizations, which allow firms to gain competitive advantage over competitors outside the network. Network members are not completely dependent on each other – as in the case of vertical integration – but the relationships established among the firms are still essential for their own final competitive position.

After these initial contributions, there has been increasing interest in strategic networks of firms from both academics and policy-makers. Initially, the majority focused mainly upon the causes and consequences of alliances at a dyadic level (Larson 1992) that is a firm-to-firm alliance, while a few began developing a branch of research aimed at looking at the social network in which firms are embedded.

Gulati (1998) introduces a 'social' perspective to business network studies. He goes beyond the dyadic level and analyzes strategic alliances among firms within a wider network context, highlighting how relationships can affect both the behaviours and performance of companies. He defines strategic networks as networks composed of inter-organizational ties that endure and have strategic significance for the firms entering them.

In a broad sense, the concept of strategic network includes a variety of different coalitions among distinct firms (or business units), such as strategic alliances, joint ventures, long-term supplier–buyer agreements, trade associations, industrial districts, franchising and other similar agreements or contracts. In general, being part of a strategic network gives the firm access to information, resources, markets and technologies and facilitates the acquisition of advantages from economies of scale, learning and scope. Moreover it allows firms to share risk and to outsource some activities of their value chain or organizational functions. These are all advantages to which the firm, standing alone, would not have access.

As shown in Fig. 2.1, Inkpen and Tsang (2005) classified different kinds of strategic networks according to two criteria: the nature of the agreement among the partners and the position of the latter along the entire value chain.

The first dimension refers to the system of governance of the network: *structured* networks imply some form of formal agreement which links the members and reduces their freedom – such as ownership rights, contracts, rules, institutionalization of the network – while *unstructured* networks are founded on informal, spontaneous interactions and simple reciprocity.

Looking at the second dimension, on one side Inkpen and Tsang (2005) define as *vertical* those networks which gather together firms with very different profiles, covering a large range of business activities, and thus having more differentiated demands and expectations about cooperation. This is the case, for instance, of *intracorporate networks* which include distinct autonomous organizations that

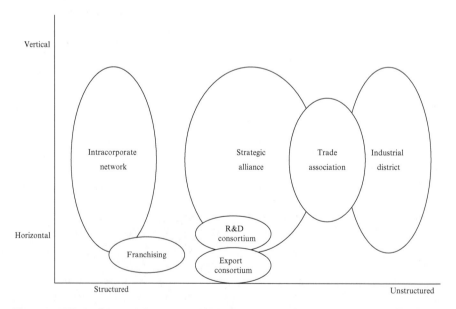

Fig. 2.1 Different forms of strategic networks (*Source*: Adapted from Inkpen and Tsang 2005)

operate under the control of a holding, or a group of subsidiaries accountable to their headquarters. Even *industrial districts*, which are composed of actors with different activities and belonging to different but related industries, are vertical local networks. This is true also of *strategic alliances* where distinct firms partially cooperate with others for specific activities, functions or common actions on the markets. On the other side, they define as *horizontal* a network which groups together firms that have a similar core business and therefore join forces to achieve a very specific goal. Horizontal networks involve firms located in the same industry segment or producing complementary products. They face similar challenges in their competitive arenas and thus may be more prone to agreeing common strategies. Examples of firms forming horizontal networks are: retailers linked in a *franchising network* who are interested in selling products by adopting a common framework; firms belonging to a *research and development consortium,* who are interested in combining their resources and competences in order to develop innovation together; members of an *export consortium*, who are interested in promoting their products abroad or entering new markets through collective actions.

As this book focuses specifically on export consortia, we restrict our analysis to the application of the concept of network to '*interfirm*' networks. An interfirm network is a group of independent organizations that interact, directly or indirectly, and is based on one or more alliances that join them. The final goal of such a network is to provide the member firms with the opportunity to increase their individual competitive advantage within the markets, ultimately building an additional competitive advantage for the entire network. Indeed, being part of a network may produce significant effects for individual member firms, many more than those produced via simple dyadic alliances, as multi-firm partnerships considerably increase the opportunities and fruits of cooperation.

We are primarily interested in '*horizontal*' interfirm networks. Ghauri et al. (2003) makes a major distinction between *vertical* and *horizontal* interfirm networks, defining the first as '*cooperative relationships between suppliers, producers and buyers, aiming at a solution for marketing problems, improved production efficiency, or the exploitation of market opportunities*', while horizontal networks are '*cooperative network relationships among manufacturers who want to solve a common marketing problem, improve production efficiency, or exploit a market opportunity through resource mobilization and sharing*'. Export consortia belong to this second type of network. In particular, we focus upon horizontal interfirm networks *among SMEs*, which present peculiarities compared to networks involving large firms, due to the specific characteristics of small business management and entrepreneurship.

Nowadays there is considerable literature dealing specifically with networks among SMEs. In the mid to late 1980s, in fact, scholars also began to apply the network perspective to the study of entrepreneurship and small business (Conway and Jones 2006).

Some scholars focused on industrial districts and clusters of SMEs, exploring the phenomenon of collaborative arrangements between local firms and their impact on the competitiveness of the cluster (Piore and Sabel 1984; Pyke 1992). In doing so, they also underlined the special role often played by third parties – such as local chambers of commerce, development agencies or business associations – to serve as a catalyst for small business networking. Other scholars, however, focused on the social networks of single entrepreneurs and the impact of their interpersonal and social ties with external actors upon the ability to create and develop their own business (Aldrich et al. 1986; Aldrich and Zimmer 1986; Birley 1985).

Human and Provan (1997) define SME networks as '*intentionally formed group of small and medium sized profit-oriented companies, in which the firms are geographically proximate, operate within the same industry, potentially sharing inputs and outputs and undertake direct interactions with each other for specific business outcomes*'. Proximity is a condition that enables firms to efficiently exchange or combine resources and competences, while being part of the same industry – in a broad sense – allows them to develop synergies along their value chain.

Stable interfirm networks allow members to gain reciprocal access to resources controlled by their partners. By relying on resource sharing and the coordination of production processes, firms can achieve economies of scale and scope, and simultaneously avoid the disadvantages of full organizational integration, such as high coordination costs and less strategic flexibility. In addition, by working more closely with other firms, an SME can access and share expertise, resources and knowledge in ways that would be impossible independently. In particular, tacit knowledge is transferred in relationships and, as this requires direct and personal interactions, it is more likely to take place in highly cooperative relationships (Welch et al. 1996). It is worth noting that in such networks cooperation is not necessarily always direct and wide. Members remain independent companies (they may also be competitors in the same markets) and in many cases they prefer to cooperate with other participating firms only when they judge it necessary.

Export consortia are typical examples of horizontal networks of SMEs and make it possible to loosen the constraints related to the investments needed to penetrate foreign markets. They are also domestic networks, in the sense that they involve SMEs of only one country, characterized by complementary and mutually-enhancing offers, which cooperate to develop higher-value products and services for their customers.

2.3 SMEs and Competitiveness: The Relational Perspective

The main contribution of the social network approach to the study of small firms lies in the current belief that comprehensive explanations of SME competitiveness (at both domestic and international level) must include the context of relationships through which small entrepreneurs obtain information, resources and social support. Indeed, the structural fragility of many small firms can be offset by the supportive environment provided by the network. This contributes to the generation of an organizing context around the member firms which helps entrepreneurs cope with ambiguity, uncertainty and lack of resources and information. It acts in a positive way not just during the start-up stage of a firm's lifecycle, but also over the subsequent stages of growth.

Until the 1990s, however, the network construct faced many difficulties in entering the field of strategy, as it did not fit into the prominent paradigm of competition based on microeconomic theory.

Scholars of business strategy had always focused on the analysis of the differential firm performance, seeking to understand the sources of competitive advantage and the causes of the supernormal returns of successful firms.

Traditionally, two principal explanations have emerged. The first, known as the *industry-based view,* sustains that the supernormal returns achieved by successful firms depend on their ability to understand the structural conditions of their industry, to deal with the dynamics of competition within it – such as bargaining power and entry barriers – and to place themselves in the most advantageous position within the given environment (Porter 1980, 1985). As a consequence of its underlying assumptions, this view sees industry as the fundamental unit of analysis for designing the competitive strategy of the firm. Conversely, the second view, known as the *resource-based view,* assumes that the profit differentials between firms are more probably due to the heterogeneity of the firms than to the structure of the industry. This is because only firms which succeed in accumulating rare, valuable, difficult-to-replicate and difficult-to-imitate resources and competences will be able to achieve a competitive advantage (Amit and Schoemaker 1993; Barney 1991; Grant 1991, 1996). This approach considers the firm as the primary unit of analysis for strategy-making.

Over the last three decades, the diffusion of alliances among firms has highlighted the strategic relevance of dyadic relations and networks for firm performance. The key question is whether or not such a cooperative strategy may produce additional competitive advantage for the individual firms involved. In fact, although they make a substantial contribution to the understanding of the supernormal profits of a firm, neither of the traditional analysis perspectives (*industry-based* or *resource-based*), consider the benefits obtained from exchanges with partners.

In order to highlight the relevance of alliances and networks in building sustainable competitive advantages for the firms, scholars have adopted terms such as '*collaborative advantage*' (Kanter 1994), '*organizational advantage*' (Nahapiet and Ghoshal 1998) or '*interorganizational competitive advantage*' (Dyer and Singh 1998).

Furthermore, in the specific field of entrepreneurship and small business management studies, some scholars have argued that both industry-based and resource-based approaches alone are inadequate in explaining the conduct of small firms. This is because SMEs are usually strongly embedded in networks of social relations (Aldrich and Zimmer 1986). Entrepreneurs live the apparent paradox of being economic actors characterized by a strong sense of autonomy and independence, while at the same time, the outcomes of their activity are often substantially affected by ties with the environment and cooperation with external actors (Johannisson and Peterson 1984).

For all these reasons, in addition to the two traditional perspectives on competitive advantage, it seems appropriate to consider a third research perspective: *the relational view*. The relational view assumes the network to be a significant unit of analysis in order to understand the supernormal profitability of firms. In other words, the network can be seen as a potential source of additional advantage for SMEs because of the value produced by the links among firms.

2.4 The Relevance of Social Capital Within the Network

The focus of the relational perspective of analysis lies in the concept of 'social capital', created by and within the network, which is used by researchers to indicate the source of various benefits that networks bring to their member firms.

Social capital in business is defined as *'the sum of the actual and potential resources embedded within, available through and derived from the network of relationships possessed by an individual or a social unit'* (Nahapiet and Ghoshal 1998). This particular set of resources, embedded in the network, promotes the creation and exchange of 'intellectual capital' (knowledge and knowing capabilities) among the partners. In its turn, 'intellectual capital' provides the firms with an additional *organizational advantage* that makes them better able to compete on the markets. In other words, an interfirm network can place social capital at the firms' disposal, supporting the production of intellectual capital (capabilities for creating and transferring knowledge), which ultimately fosters the competitive advantage of firms.

Social capital is a complex construct. Nahapiet and Ghoshal (1998) – reassessing the findings of several authors, including Coleman (1988, 1990), Putnam (1995) and Granovetter (1992) define its nature in a comprehensive model which identifies three inter-related dimensions of social capital: *structural, relational* and *cognitive*.

The *structural dimension of social capital* refers to the patterns of connections between actors: the number and kinds of actors involved; the presence or absence of direct ties between specific individual actors; the configuration and morphology of the network in terms of density, connectivity and hierarchy, and the stability of ties between nodes. By analyzing the structure of existing relationships, it is possible to understand the channels of communication and exchanges between nodes. The *relational dimension of social capital* focuses on the behavioural assets of the network (created and leveraged by members through relationships) such as trust and trustworthiness, norms and sanctions, obligations and expectations, identity and identification. From this we discern to what extent the partners are ready and prone to exchange knowledge. Finally, the *cognitive dimension of social capital* refers to those resources providing shared representations, interpretations, language and codes, narratives and, in general, a common system of meanings among partners. These aspects allow not only communication, but also, more generally, the transfer of knowledge between the nodes of the network.

The presence of a strong social capital within the network increases the efficiency of the actions of the network, diminishes the probability of opportunism and reduces the need for costly monitoring processes. It constitutes a necessary requirement for producing significant benefits for firms when they are united on the market, both domestic and international.

Small entrepreneurs accumulate social capital in networks that support their pursuit of growth opportunities, including internationalization. The information, knowledge and resources that may be useful in exploring foreign markets are generally drawn from the formal and informal contacts that entrepreneurs establish outside their organization.

In interfirm networks, the competitive advantage of each firm is linked to the advantages of the network of relationships in which the firm is embedded, as these relationships may provide valuable 'rents' for both the network and the member firms. However, the creation, maintenance and development of social capital within a network is a costly task. The process of forming and exploiting the social capital requires investment and time. Furthermore, the process is subject to constant (but not necessarily rational and well-informed) assessment of its relative costs and benefits by the network members.

2.5 Networks as Sources of Competitive Advantage

Once we acknowledge that social capital can generate 'relational rents' for network members, the next question is to understand *how* this happens, that is, what the actual sources of the additional advantage produced by network connections are.

Dyer and Singh (1998) focus on network routines and processes as sources of the emergence of an inter-organizational advantage, examining how relational rents are earned and preserved in alliances and networks. They define relational rent as '*a supernormal profit jointly generated in an exchange relationship that cannot be generated by either the firm in isolation and can only be created through the joint idiosyncratic contributions of the specific alliance partners*' (Dyer and Singh 1998).

According to these authors, the production of relational rents within a network may have four main determinants: *investments in relation-specific assets*; *knowledge sharing routines* within the network; the combination of *complementary resources and capabilities* among the partners, and the adoption of an *effective system of governance of the network*.

Firstly, relational rents depend on the investments policy adopted by the network: *The greater the investment by partners is, in relation-specific assets (both in physical or human assets), the greater the potential will be for relational rents*. By the term 'relation specific', Dyer and Singh (1998) mean specific investments in, for example, machinery, tools or dies, or in dedicated personnel, development of know-how or routines that are employed specifically for the activities of the network. Common investments by the network members in such areas produce two main benefits. On the one hand, the necessity to guarantee returns on the investment during a payback period lengthens the safeguard of the alliance and protects against opportunistic behaviour. On the other, common investments allow greater exchanges among partners and facilitate interfirm cooperation, thereby enhancing performance.

Secondly, networks can generate rents by developing superior interfirm knowledge-sharing routines – regular patterns of interaction that permit the transfer, combination or creation of specialized knowledge among firms: *the greater the investment in interfirm knowledge-sharing routines, the greater the potential will be for relational rents.* Such interfirm routines promote know-how and information exchange among network members, but they also require the individual firms to have 'absorptive capacity' (Cohen and Levinthal 1990). This is the capacity to recognize the value of external information, assimilate it and apply it to business operations. In order to effectively obtain knowledge transfer, firms must be encouraged to be transparent, while not freeloading with know-how acquired from their partners.

Thirdly, relational rents derive from the combination of the partners' resources and competences which – due to emerging synergies – collectively generate greater rents than the sum of those that could be obtained from each firm: *the greater the extent of valuable, synergy-sensitive, rare, difficult-to-imitate resources owned by network members, the greater the potential will be to generate relational rents.* By combining such complementary resources or capabilities of its members, the network will develop a stronger competitive advantage than that achievable by the individual firms operating independently. Of course, this 'complementing' of the resources and competences of member firms depends on the profiles of partners as well as on the alignment of their organizational cultures and strategies. Therefore the selection of partners is crucial for the success of the network.

Finally, governance of the network plays a key role in the creation of relational rents: *the greater the ability of member firms to minimize transaction costs and maximize the value of their exchanges, the greater the potential will be for relational rents.* The first consequence of effective governance mechanisms is to enhance the efficiency of the network in terms of lowering transaction costs. In a well-governed network, lower transaction costs derive from favourable conditions in the interaction among partners. They trust that payoffs will be divided fairly; apply a low-cost mechanism of self-monitoring; are more flexible in adjusting their agreement to respond to external changes, and are not subject to the time limitations typical of formal contracts. Moreover, effective mechanisms of governance may generate relational rents not only by simply lowering transaction costs, but also by affecting each of the other three sources of rents. In fact, the governance mechanisms affect the relation-specific investments made by the network, the knowledge which will be shared, and the choice of capability matching among different partners.

Networks enable their member firms to access valuable know-how in two main ways. Firstly, they can facilitate the transfer of knowledge from one firm to another, acting as a conduit for processing and moving resources and information between the nodes. Secondly, networks themselves can become the locus of new knowledge development.

With particular reference to the knowledge transfer process within the partners of a network, Inkpen and Tsang (2005) sustain that social capital plays a critical role in such a process, and that conditions facilitating this transfer are strongly associated with the facets of the three dimensions of social capital (*structural, cognitive, relational*).

Concerning the *structural dimension*, for instance, knowledge transfer is facilitated by strong ties and repeated exchanges among the nodes, as well as by the physical proximity of member firms, stable personal relationships, the existence of multiple connections among partners (i.e. working simultaneously on a variety of projects or occasions in experimental cooperation) and by a non-competitive approach to knowledge transfer.

As far as the *cognitive dimension* is concerned, knowledge transfer is facilitated by the adoption of norms and rules to govern informal knowledge exchange and by goal clarity among partners. A shared vision and defined strategic objectives reduce conflicts and aid negotiation.

Finally, regarding the *relational dimension*, there is fairly clear evidence that when knowledge sharing is embedded in social ties, the risk of opportunistic behaviour is limited. Therefore, when relationships between firms are embedded with trust, the transfer of distinctive knowledge and valuable resources is more likely to be smooth and effective.

This argument definitively introduces into our discussion the topic of 'trust' in interfirm networks, and underlines the extent to which trust-building between entrepreneurs is crucial, since SME networks usually '*do not emerge without considerable endeavour*' (Birley et al. 1991: 58).

2.6 Trust as a Requirement for Building Successful SME Networks[1]

Alliance and network building among SMEs is far from being a simple task. Due to the high probability of conflict among entrepreneurs – who often have individualistic and "masculine" profiles – achieving the goal of collaboration can be a complex and risky venture (Medcof 1997). In such a context, the *development of trust* among alliance members has been widely recognized as a fundamental issue for establishing effective relational ties (Parkhe 1998; Zaheer et al. 1998).

The topic of trust has been analyzed from several perspectives, within such disciplines as psychology, sociology and economics. With regard to the latter, over the last two decades a growing amount of attention has been paid to the subject of trust among actors within the same and different organizations (Dirks and Ferrin 2001; Gulati 1995; Krishnan et al. 2006; Saparito et al. 2004; Zaheer and Harris 2006; Zaheer et al. 1998).

---

[1] This section and Sect. 2.7 largely benefit from the work by Cannatelli and Antoldi (2010).

Zaheer et al. (1998) define trust as *'the expectation that an actor can be relied on to fulfil obligations, will behave in a predictable manner, and will act and negotiate fairly when the possibility for opportunism is present'*. Their research highlights the need to distinguish between interpersonal and inter-organizational trust. The individual 'boundary spanner' at a single firm establishes relationships with both individuals and groups of individuals belonging to the partner organization. Hence, if the origin of the relationship is always an individual, the counterpart may vary. This insight is very useful in avoiding the cross-level fallacy (Russeau 1985), for one can then distinguish between these two levels of analysis. This insight has been of great value, especially in examining the relationships among SMEs which are prone to an overlap of interpersonal and inter-organizational ties.

In accordance with this approach, trust among partners has a significant impact on the respective firm's performance by reducing transaction costs and conflicts. In fact, other benefits, such as increased sales and a greater return on investment, may also be identified as direct outcomes of trust (Luo 2002; Mohr and Spekman 1994; Zaheer and Harris 2006).

Trust should be enhanced by network members in response to three main constraints which discourage small firms from establishing long-term collaboration agreements: (a) the risk of opportunism among the entrepreneurs, (b) low commitment from counterparts and (c) the culture of the actors joining an alliance.

The risk of *opportunism* derives from the divergence of objectives and management styles of the firms involved, as well as from environmental volatility. Williamson (1975) defined it as 'self-interest seeking with guile'. Opportunism increases the complexity of the alliance-building process by increasing the transaction costs, reducing confidence levels among participants, and by focusing on short-term rather than long-term interest, thus discouraging reciprocity and repeated commitment (Luo 2002; Parkhe 1998).

A high level of *commitment* is necessary for a successful strategy in a firm as well as in a strategic alliance. According to Salancik (1977), commitment represents the binding of an individual to behavioural acts, and Ghemawat (1991) defines it as the tendency towards the persistence of a firm's strategy, underlining its relevance in producing superior performance. Conversely, alliances characterized by the low commitment of its members – due to important differences in self-interest, business characteristics and market strategies – may collapse, owing to substantial differences between the firms in the amount of time and resources invested (Medcof 1997).

Finally, the individual *culture* of the entrepreneurs joining the alliance plays an important role in determining their attitude to participation in the collective strategies (Xiaohua 2007). Hofstede defines culture as 'the collective programming of the mind which distinguishes the members of one human group from another' (Hofstede 2001). Accordingly, masculine, individualistic cultures tend to act as a barrier to considering a competitor as a potential partner, while 'feminine', collective cultures seem to correlate to cooperation.

As anticipated, trust challenges the above-mentioned constraints by laying the foundation for a common ground, where entrepreneurs can successfully meet their expectations (Ring and Van de Ven 1992; Zaheer and Harris 2006).

Before analyzing the emergence of trust within the network, it is necessary to introduce the topic of *rationality* and its role in leading entrepreneurs to the decision of whether or not to join an alliance. In order to broaden the topic, it is useful to refer to the debate about the relationship between *calculativeness,* which usually focuses on the economic returns of a decision, and *trust,* which focuses more on the psychological and social dimensions of behaviour.

Different statements have been made about the relationship that occurs between the two paradigms, especially when referring to issues associated with an alliance. Some authors consider calculativeness as a component of the trust-building process among the economic actors, and therefore include the economic expedience of an alliance as an ingredient of trust (Doney et al. 1998; Luo 2002; Zaheer and Venkatraman 1995). Conversely, according to Williamson (1993), calculativeness is the only paradigm that is in a position to explain economic behaviour, asserting that trust '*is reserved for very special relations between family, friends and lovers*'. Hence, he goes on to state that '*calculative trust is a contradiction in terms*'. Such a position has been strongly objected to by Craswell (1993). Like Williamson, Craswell considers calculativeness and trust to be two separate concepts. However, he diverges from Williamson's view in conceiving the two paradigms to be complementary rather than mutually exclusive.

2.7 The Role of 'Network Facilitators': An Interpretative Framework

Despite the evident trust-related benefits for small firms that decide to join a network, trust among small entrepreneurs is rarely a naturally-occurring phenomenon. In networks composed of SMEs, trust often emerges over time as a result of both frequent interactions between entrepreneurs and the specific activities conducted by third parties acting as 'trust or network facilitators'. More specifically, the topic of network facilitator is relevant for export consortia of SMEs, which are usually created via the initiative of third parties.

Such entities are usually individuals or organizations that leverage their reputation and abilities by facilitating interfirm relationships within a local cluster or group of firms. Their role is to promote and strengthen relationships among firms, give a clear strategy to the alliance, mediate negotiations among partners and help network members create opportunities for trust, shifting them out of their collaborative inertia (Mesquita 2007).

Examples of these facilitators in industrialized countries include local business associations, local banks, chambers of commerce, educational and training institutions, private consultants, local development agencies or public government bodies (at central or local level). Their role has often been often crucial both in the creation and development of industrial districts and clusters, and in the start-up of networks and consortia of SMEs. In developing countries – where local environments are usually not rich in resources or self-organized initiatives – this role may also be played by special government agencies, specialized development banks (such as the World Bank or Banco Interamericano de Desarollo), non-governmental organizations or multilateral international agencies (such as UNIDO – the United Nations Industrial Development Organization). International agencies usually have their own specific programmes and operate through joint co-financed projects in the field, aimed at starting and promoting clusters or networks of SMEs (see the nine case histories in Chaps. 4 and 5).

When acting as network facilitators, not all these actors can be strictly defined as third parties. Sometimes – particularly when they are local actors – they are deeply embedded in the social structure and the ties between them, and the SMEs are long-lasting. In some cases (for instance when the facilitator is a public actor) their presence is crucial in order to obtain financial resources. The network facilitator acts as a (formal or informal) leader of the network and can be considered a constitutive part of the alliance in all respects.

Conversely, the nine export consortia that we analyzed in Morocco, Tunisia, Peru and Uruguay were all promoted and supported by an international agency, namely UNIDO, which is an external actor, not part of the network. In all these cases (see Chap. 4) the network facilitator really is a third party compared to the entrepreneurs involved. In other words, the facilitator is not embedded in the network, has no direct interest in the business and, therefore, acts within a temporary perspective. In fact, the final goal of the network facilitator is to enable the network members, in the medium term, to operate autonomously. Leveraging on public funds and on its international know-how, UNIDO accompanies and supports the start-up and development of the network, but all those involved in the projects are aware from the beginning that the network facilitator's support of the smaller firms will sooner or later cease. This condition has an important consequence: the strategic time horizon of the network is longer than the intervention timetable of network facilitator.

The concept of network facilitator was introduced by McEvily and Zaheer (2004) in order to analyze the role of institutions in fostering collaboration among actors involved in geographical industrial networks. More in particular, these authors define these facilitators as 'Architects of Trust', focusing on the dynamic through which trust is built among individuals belonging to geographically close organizations involved in the alliance. The main result of their study has been a better understanding of the importance of a third party that is trusted by each participant due to the existence of a pre-existing relationship.

Despite the fact that network facilitators clearly play a relevant role in building trust among participants (Obstfeld 2005), how this actually occurs is still unclear, especially from a longitudinal perspective.

Figure 2.2 presents a three-stage model that describes the evolutionary pattern of an alliance among SMEs in the form of a network (Cannatelli and Antoldi 2010). Four elements of analysis are included: (a) the time perspective adopted by partners in building their alliance; (b) the main cohesive factor that links partners in different

2.7 The Role of 'Network Facilitators': An Interpretative Framework

	STAGE 1	STAGE 2	STAGE 3
Time perspective	**Short** term perspective	**Short** term perspective	**Long** term perspective
Cohesive factor	First contact among entrepreneurs Identification of a **business opportunity**. *Calculativeness (not trust)*	Time for **bridging relationships** Emerging of social capital. *Mediated trust*	Identify with members and territory. Emerging of an **alliance identity**. *Relational trust*
Business objective	Share a business **opportunity**	Build **trust** and share **knowledge**	Share a **market strategy**
Mission of network facilitator	Rationalizing the business opportunity, weaving the alliance *(dyadic relationships with each member)*	Fostering communication and knowledge transfer among entrepreneurs Alliance warrantor	Handing over the control of the alliance to an internal leader, being an external source of support

CALCULATIVENESS → CALCULATIVENESS + TRUST

Fig. 2.2 Stages of evolution in strategic networks (*Source*: Adapted from Cannatelli and Antoldi 2010)

moments of their collaboration; (c) the strategic objective of the alliance; (d) the functions carried out by the network facilitator at different stages.

The starting point in the early stage of the model is the presence of a cohesive factor among partners which can consist of a business opportunity for firms. This opportunity may emerge in different forms, such as the presence of a potential collective deal, the availability of special public funds, a common state of crisis for the firms or a particular political context that motivates entrepreneurs to join forces.

The main feature of this cohesive factor is that it must be 'catalyzing', i.e. it is able to attract potential members to the alliance. According to the calculativeness paradigm cited above, the decision to start cooperation is considered a product of the calculative process that measures the convenience of an action by comparing goals and resources. Hence, in the early stage, the objective of the cooperation is to seize a business opportunity.

In the second stage, the activities required by the common project (such as meetings to assess the production capacity and quality standards within the network, or to select the target markets) bridge relationships among members, and knowledge begins to flow, albeit informally. According to Anderson and Narus (1990), at this stage the relationship among entrepreneurs changes, going beyond the original ground of cooperation (the cohesive factor) and moving towards an embryonic form of trust that is still mediated by the network facilitator.

The perspective assumed in this framework considers trust and calculativeness to be different but linked concepts, complementary categories of rationality, rather than simply alternatives. In so doing, this leaves the door open to an entrepreneurial decision-making process in which calculative, psychological and sociological elements coexist.

Finally, in the third stage, a personal assessment by each entrepreneur of the level of convenience (both economic and social) of the alliance will emerge. This assessment is helpful in strengthening relationships and facilitating the development of trust among members. The need to feel part of a group is proven by the signs of identification that begin to develop. At this point, the path from a fully calculative to a relational trust approach reaches maturity.

There is a correlation between (a) the stage of the alliance, (b) the dimension of rationality and (c) the time perspective adopted by members. It appears that the early stages of network creation are strictly connected to a calculative approach. The fear of opportunistic behaviour by potential partners has emerged in the literature as being an important obstacle to alliance formation, especially in the partner selection task (Holmberg and Cummings 2009). Accordingly, the first stage of the framework is characterized by a short-term collaboration perspective, while in the later stages – when the entrepreneurs' personal assessment becomes not merely economic, but also social – the time perspective evolves into the 'long-run'.

The passages from one stage to the next lead to significant changes in the tasks of the network facilitator. It is important to focus on two features related to the role of the network facilitator within a strategic alliance: the *position* assumed and the *activities* carried out by said institution in each of the three stages of network creation.

The most critical characteristic of the network facilitator to emerge during the first stage of the alliance is its *pivotal* position. This can be seen as a consequence of three facts: the network facilitator is the actor who maintains control over the cohesive factor (market opportunity); the network facilitator is the only actor within the network directly connected to each other member; the network facilitator is seen as trustworthy by each entrepreneur, due to its neutrality.

As illustrated in Fig. 2.3, by virtue of the dyadic relationships that the network facilitator holds with each entrepreneur and the absence of ties between the other members, the usual position of the network facilitator in the first stage is pivotal. In this early stage the contribution of the network facilitator, in terms of activities, is to identify the business opportunity, making it accessible for the firms; to design the framework for cooperation; to coordinate activities (as the pivot of the alliance) and keep the cohesive factor achievable.

In the second stage, because of the trust relationships that exist between the network facilitator and the members, its position remains central, even if these relationships cease to be exclusive; loose ties between firms begin to take shape. However, as the guarantor of the entrepreneurs' behaviour with other members, the presence of the network facilitator is still critical, and its role could be defined as *mediator*. The activities conducted in this stage are mainly oriented towards the facilitating of relationship development among members, making the dialogue between them as smooth as possible.

In the final stage the trust among members reaches maturity. Ties are strengthened from the knowledge transfer and common experiences gained in previous

2.7 The Role of 'Network Facilitators': An Interpretative Framework

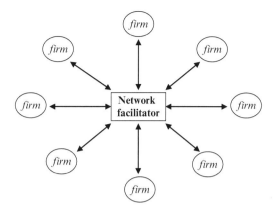

Stage 1 – Network facilitator as *Pivot of the alliance*

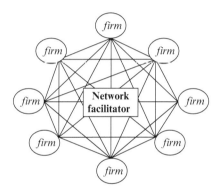

Stage 2 - Network facilitator as *Mediator of the alliance*

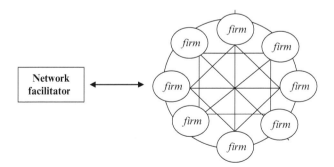

Stage 3 - Network facilitator as *Advisor of the alliance*

Fig. 2.3 The role played by the Network facilitator over time (*Source*: Adapted from Cannatelli and Antoldi 2010)

years. In this way, the need for a guarantor gradually decreases, as each entrepreneur freely decides to trust other members of the alliance. As such, the network will no longer need an internal facilitator. Rather, it will cast aside the mediator position in favour of an internal leadership that ensures that entrepreneurial guidance is in place for the alliance. Nevertheless, the activities carried out during this stage – where the facilitator assumes the position of *advisor* – are designed to encourage the alliance to build an internal leadership and to support the firms externally, by continuously seeking out opportunities and watching over relationships.

The chief role of the network facilitator appears to be one of fostering trust within the strategic alliance. When calculativeness is at the core of the interest, the facilitator offers a cohesive factor which makes it attractive for members to cooperate in order to receive economic benefits from the collaboration. However, when the cohesive factor ceases to be exclusively an economic opportunity, and as members become more willing to cooperate (as a result of trust), the facilitator needs to begin to move away from the alliance while still guaranteeing support when needed.

References

Aldrich, H. E., & Zimmer, C. (1986). Entrepreneurship through social networks. In D. L. Sexton & R. W. Wilson (Eds.), *The art and science of entrepreneurship* (pp. 154–167). Cambridge, MA: Ballinger.

Aldrich, H. E., Rose, B., & Woodward, W. (1986). Social behaviour and entrepreneurial networks. In R. Ronstadt, J. A. Hornaday, R. Peterson, & K. H. Vesper (Eds.), *Frontiers of entrepreneurship research* (pp. 239–241). Wellessley, MA: Babson College.

Amit, R., & Schoemaker, P. (1993). Strategic assets & organizational rent. *Strategic Management Journal, 14*(1), 33–46.

Anderson, J. C., & Narus, J. A. (1990). A model of distributor firm and manufacturer firm working partnership. *The Journal of Marketing, 54*(1), 42–58.

Barney, J. B. (1991). Firm resources and sustained competitive advantage. *Journal of Management, 17*(1), 99–120.

Birley, S. (1985). The role of networks in the entrepreneurial process. *Journal of Business Venturing, 1*(1), 107–117.

Birley, S., Cromie, S., & Myers, A. (1991). Entrepreneurial networks: Their emergence in Ireland and Overseas. *International Small Business Journal, 9*(4), 56–74.

Cannatelli, B., & Antoldi, F. (2010, June). *Fostering trust within strategic alliances among SMEs: A study on the role of network facilitator*. Paper presented at 2010 World Conference of International Council for Small Business (pp. 24–27), Cincinnati, Ohio.

Chetty, S., & Agndal, H. (2007). Social capital and its influence on changes in internationalization mode among small and medium-sized enterprises. *Journal of International Marketing, 15*(1), 1–29.

Cohen, W. M., & Levinthal, D. A. (1990). Absorptive capacity: A new perspective on learning and innovation. *Administrative Science Quarterly, 35*(1), 128–152.

Coleman, J. S. (1988). Social capital in the creation of human capital. *The American Journal of Sociology, 94*(Suppl), S95–S120.

Coleman, J. S. (1990). *Foundations of social theory*. Cambridge, MA: Harvard University Press.

Conway, S., & Jones, O. (2006). Networking and the small business. In S. Carter & D. Jones-Evans (Eds.), *Enterprise and small business*. Harlow: Prentice Hall.

References

Conway, S., Jones, O., & Steward, F. (2001). Realising the potential of the social network perspective in innovation studies. In O. Jones, S. Comway, & F. Steward (Eds.), *Social interaction and organisational change: Aston perspectives on innovation networks* (pp. 349–366). London: Imperial College Press.

Coviello, N. E., & Munro, H. J. (1995). Growing the entrepreneurial firm: Networking for international market development. *European Journal of Marketing, 29*(7), 49–61.

Coviello, N. E., & Munro, H. J. (1997). Network relationships and the internationalisation process of small software firms. *International Business Review, 6*(4), 361–386.

Craswell, R. (1993). On the uses of 'trust': Comment on Williamson, 'Calculativeness, Trust, and Economic Organization'. *The Journal of Law & Economics, 36*(1), 487.

Cruickshank, P., & Rolland, D. (2006). Entrepreneurial success through networks and social capital: Exploratory considerations from gem research in New Zealand. *Journal of Small Business and Entrepreneurship, 19*(1), 63–80.

Dirks, K. T., & Ferrin, D. L. (2001). The role of trust in organizational settings. *Organization Science, 12*(4), 450–467.

Doney, P. M., Cannon, J. P., & Mullen, M. (1998). Understanding the influence of national culture on the development of trust. *The Academy of Management Review, 23*(3), 601–620.

Doz, Y. L., & Hamel, G. (1998). *Alliance advantage: The art of creating value through partnering*. Boston: Harvard Business Press.

Dyer, J. H., & Singh, H. (1998). The relational view: Cooperative strategy and sources of interorganizational competitive advantage. *The Academy of Management Review, 23*(4), 660–679.

Ghauri, P., Lutz, C., & Tesfom, G. (2003). Using networks to solve export-marketing problems of small- and medium-sized firms from developing countries. *European Journal of Marketing, 37*(5/6), 728–752.

Ghemawat, P. (1991). *Commitment: The dynamic of strategy*. New York: Free Press.

Granovetter, M. S. (1992). Problems of explanation in economic sociology. In N. Nohria & R. Eccles (Eds.), *Networks and organizations: Structure, form and action* (pp. 25–56). Boston: Harvard Business Press.

Grant, R. M. (1991). The resource-based theory of competitive advantage: Implications for strategy formulation. *California Management Review, 33*(3), 114–135.

Grant, R. M. (1996). Toward a knowledge-based theory of the firm. *Strategic Management Journal, 17*, 109–122. Special Issue: Knowledge and the firm.

Gulati, R. (1995). Does familiarity breed trust? The implications of repeated ties for contractual choice in alliances. *Academy of Management Journal, 38*(1), 85–112.

Gulati, R. (1998). Alliances and networks. *Strategic Management Journal, 19*(4), 293–317.

Hofstede, G. (2001). *Culture's consequence, comparing values, behaviours, institutions and organizations across nations*. Thousand Oaks, CA: Sage Publications.

Holmberg, S. R., & Cummings, J. L. (2009). Building success full strategic alliances: Strategic process and analytical tool for selecting partner industries and firms. *Long Range Planning, 42*(2), 164–193.

Hoskisson, R. E., Eden, L., Lau, C.-M., & Wright, M. (2000). Strategy in emerging economies. *Academy of Management Journal, 43*(3), 249–267.

Human, S. E., & Provan, K. G. (1997). An emerging theory of structure and outcomes in small-firms strategic manufacturing networks. *Academy of Management Journal, 40*, 386–403.

Inkpen, A. C., & Tsang, E. W. K. (2005). Social capital, networks and knowledge transfer. *The Academy of Management Review, 30*(1), 46–165.

Jarillo, J. C. (1988). On strategic networks. *Strategic Management Journal, 9*(1), 31–41.

Johannisson, B. (1987). Anarchists and organisers: entrepreneurs in a network perspective. *International Studies of Management and Organizations, XVII*(1), 49–63.

Johannisson, B. (2000). Networking and entrepreneurial growth. In D. Sexton & H. Landstrom (Eds.), *Handbook of entrepreneurship*. Oxford: Blackwell.

Johannisson, B., & Peterson, R. (1984). *The personal networks of entrepreneurs.* Paper presented at the Third Canadian Conference of the International Council for Small Business, Toronto (pp. 23–25).

Kanter, R. M. (1994). Collaborative advantage. *Harvard Business Review*, July-August.

Krishnan, R., Martin, X., & Noorderhaven, N. G. (2006). When does trust matter to alliance performance? *Academy of Management Journal, 49*(5), 894–917.

Larson, A. (1992). Network dyads in entrepreneurial settings: A study of the governance of exchange relationships. *Administrative Science Quarterly, 37*, 76–104. March.

Luo, Y. (2002). Contract, cooperation, and performance in international joint ventures. *Strategic Management Journal, 23*(10), 903–919.

Manev, I. M., Gyoshev, B. S., & Manolova, T. S. (2005). The role of human and social capital and entrepreneurial orientation for small business performance in a transition economy. *International Journal of Innovation and Entrepreneurship Management, 5*(3/4), 298–318.

Manolova, T., Brush, C., Edelman, L., & Greene, P. (2002). Internationalization of small firms: Personal factors revisited. *International Small Business Journal, 20*(1), 9–30.

McEvily, B., & Zaheer, A. (2004). Architects of trust: The role of network facilitators in geographical clusters. In R. M. Kramer & K. S. Cook (Eds.), *Trust and distrust in organizations* (pp. 189–213). New York: Russel Sage Foundation.

Medcof, J. W. (1997). Why too many alliances end in divorce. *Long Range Planning, 30*(5), 718–732.

Mesquita, L. F. (2007). Starting over when the bickering never ends: Rebuilding aggregate trust among clustered firms through trust facilitator. *The Academy of Management Review, 32*(1), 72–91.

Mesquita, L. F., & Lazzarini, S. G. (2008). Horizontal and vertical relationships in developing economies: Implications for SMEs' access to global markets. *Academy of Management Journal, 51*(2), 359–380.

Mohr, J., & Spekman, R. (1994). Characteristics of partnership success: Partnership attributes, communication behaviour, and conflict resolution techniques. *Strategic Management Journal, 15*(2), 135–152.

Nahapiet, J., & Ghoshal, S. (1998). Social capital, intellectual capital and the organizational advantage. *The Academy of Management Review, 23*(2), 242–266.

Obstfeld, D. (2005). Social networks, the Tertius Iungens orientation, and involvement in innovation. *Administrative Science Quarterly, 51*(1), 100–130.

Parkhe, A. (1998). Understanding trust in international alliances. *Journal of World Business, 33*(3), 219–240.

Piore, M., & Sabel, C. (1984). *The second industrial divide.* New York: Basic Book.

Porter, M. E. (1980). *Competitive strategy: Techniques for analysing industries and competitors.* New York: Free Press.

Porter, M. E. (1985). *Competitive advantage: Creating and sustaining superior performance.* New York: Free Press.

Putnam, R. D. (1995). Bowling alone: America's declining social capital. *Journal of Democracy, 6*(1), 65–78.

Pyke, E. (1992). *Industrial development through small firm cooperation.* Geneva: International Labour Office.

Ring, P. S., & Van De Ven, A. H. (1992). Structuring cooperative relationships between organizations. *Strategic Management Journal, 13*(7), 483–498.

Rosenfeld, S. A. (1996). Does cooperation enhance competitiveness? Assessing the impacts of interfirm collaboration. *Research Policy, 25*(2), 247–263.

Russeau, D. M. (1985). Issues of level in organizational research. In L. L. Cummings & B. M. Staw (Eds.), *Research in organizational behaviou* (pp. 1–37). Greenwich, CT: JAI Press.

Salancik, G. R. (1977). Commitment and the control of organizational behaviour and belief. In B. M. Staw & G. R. Salancik (Eds.), *New directions in organizational behaviour.* Chicago: St. Clair Press.

References

Saparito, P. A., Chen, C. C., & Sapienza, H. J. (2004). The role of relational trust in bank–small firm relationships. *Academy of Management Journal, 47*(3), 400–411.

Starr, J. A., & MacMillan, I. C. (1990). Resource cooptation via social contracting: resource acquisition strategies for new ventures. *Strategic Management Journal, 11*, 79–92. Special Issue: Corporate Entrepreneurship.

Thorelli, H. B. (1986). Between markets and hierarchies. *Strategic Management Journal, 7*(1), 37–51.

Welch, D. E., Welch, L. S., Wilkinson, I. F., & Young, L. C. (1996). Network analysis of a new export grouping scheme: The role of economic and non-economic relations. *International Journal of Research in Marketing, 13*(5), 463–477.

Williamson, O. E. (1975). *Markets and hierarchies: Analysis and antitrust implications.* New York: Free Press.

Williamson, O. E. (1993). Calculativeness, trust, and economic organization. *Journal of Law and Economics, 36*(1), 453–486.

Xiaohua, L. (2007). Chinese entrepreneurs in network marketing organizations: A culture-moderated social capital perspective. *Journal of Small Business and Entrepreneurship, 20*(3), 273–288.

Zaheer, A., & Harris, J. (2006). Interorganizational trust. In O. Shenkar & J. Reuer (Eds.), *Handbook of strategic alliances* (pp. 169–197). Thousand Oaks, CA: Sage.

Zaheer, A., & Venkatraman, N. (1995). Relational governance as an interorganizational strategy: An empirical test on the role of trust in economic exchange. *Strategic Management Journal, 16*(5), 373–392.

Zaheer, A., McEvily, B., & Perrone, V. (1998). Does trust matter? Exploring the effects of interorganizational and interpersonal trust on performance. *Organization Science, 9*(2), 141–159.

Export Consortia: Types and Characteristics

3.1 Export Consortia: An Overview

According to their differing objectives and scope, SMEs consortia may be of different types, such as research and development consortia, purchasing consortia, marketing consortia, production consortia, and export consortia.

An export consortium is '*a voluntary alliance of firms with the objective of promoting the goods and services of its members abroad and facilitating the export of these products through joint actions*' (UNIDO 2003). Export consortia therefore represent a particular form of inter-firm network dedicated to fostering the internationalization of SMEs. Forming horizontal ties with other domestic partners may enable small firms to solve a variety of internal export problems concerning the completeness and quality of the value proposition, organizational and financial issues, and the lack of information about foreign markets.

Export consortia are some of the least studied internationalization networks. However, they represent an attractive means of overcoming some barriers to export as they enable firms to pool resources that may be scarce at firm level and exploit economies of scale without losing firm flexibility. For this reason the consortium model is particularly advantageous for smaller firms, whether they are going international for the first time or trying to increase their existing degree of internationalization.

Compared to other kinds of networks, consortia are particularly helpful in the internationalization process of SMEs. They require relatively little financial investment, are not expensive in terms of human capital, are sufficiently loose (partners are still able to carry out many activities independently) and, finally, can be managed in such a way that partners need only participate in those initiatives which are of real interest to them.

The participation of SMEs in other types of business networks and cooperative agreements is often limited by financial constraints. For example, joint ventures may not be feasible for some SMEs as the money required to start up a new company and, more importantly, the investment in human capital necessary for initial development and subsequent control are frequently not available. Other types of agreement and network are often considered to be too rigid for SMEs as they greatly restrict member firms' freedom to change strategy or make alliances with other partners in order to achieve certain objectives. Consortia are organized loosely enough to allow partners to define strategies autonomously. Finally, participating in an export consortium does not usually involve taking part in all of its activities; partner firms can generally decide whether or not they wish to be involved in a particular project.

For all of these reasons, export consortia suit the needs of SMEs very well.

Export consortia support the internationalization process of their partners mainly by supplying specific services that help them increase sales abroad, become familiar with target markets, make their brands known and gather information about foreign customers and distribution channels. By pooling their resources, individual partners can better cope with the transaction costs associated with international marketing, most of which are related to collecting information.

The effective and efficient production of collective services to the partners is a crucial consortium activity for a variety of reasons.

First of all, if services provided by the consortium are insufficient in terms of effectiveness or efficiency, there is no reason for the partners to stay together. The quality and appropriateness of the services are therefore both key factors for success and potential sources of disruption.

Secondly, partners find it useful to be part of an export consortium if they are able to exploit economies of scale. However, if the number of partners is limited and they are free to decide whether or not to use a specific consortium service, there is a risk that the advantages deriving from economies of scale may not be exploited fully. This is particularly true in the case of multi-business consortia, where the partners come from different sectors and have very different needs. In order to avoid such a risk, the consortium's structure and management systems are crucial.

Although this kind of strategic network is focused specifically on export, internationalization is not the only benefit of such an alliance between SMEs. In many cases – for instance, the cases discussed in this book (see Chaps. 4 and 5) – joining an export consortium allows member firms to improve profitability, achieve productivity gains and accumulate knowledge through various types of joint action which are not directly related to export. Indeed, improvements in company management and organizational structure may be facilitated through cooperation between SMEs. The successful implementation of competitiveness-enhancing processes builds on investments in services (e.g. quality, traceability, certification, electronic accounting systems, innovative packaging, process improvements and production management), production equipment and technologies. Normally, these investments would not be affordable for individual SMEs, but may become possible through joint financial collaboration within a consortium.

Economies of scale may emerge when consortium members pool their resources for the joint acquisition of equipment, supplies and services (marketing, logistics, training, technical advice, etc.), thus achieving, as a group, increased bargaining power which allows them to obtain products and services under better conditions.

Moreover, when it comes to the joint definition and elaboration of 'production regulations' (necessary for obtaining quality certifications which represent significant gains in terms of added value) collaboration offers clear advantages. Furthermore, continual information exchange between associated SMEs concerning, for instance, production and human resource management practices, contribute directly to greater firm competitiveness.

Export consortia make it possible to boost the results of conventional company upgrading programmes, since cost reductions, economies of scale and replication effects can significantly increase the number of SMEs which benefit from modernization initiatives.

The benefits of consortia, however, also derive from the links which may arise between the individual activities of the member firms. Export consortia represent a powerful tool to strengthen the connections between member companies' value chains and to increase competitiveness. Furthermore, in an export consortium, the reinforcement of competitive advantages in export markets often goes hand in hand with the expansion of the local market share.

The importance of networks for the growth and competitiveness of SMEs has led many countries to promote consortia and other forms of networks among SMEs. Public agencies can facilitate initial networking and the development of trust between members (Welch et al. 1998). A government trade promotion agency is legitimized to act as a facilitator in helping firms become aware that relationships may contribute to the achievement of their goals. However, external incentives to create a consortium cannot replace the commitment and active participation of its members; a positive perception of the outcomes that networking can produce is a necessary precondition for the emergence and development of effective networks.

3.2 Features, Strengths and Weaknesses of Export Consortia

Export consortia can be classified on the basis of various factors (Depperu 1996; UNIDO 2003): scope, objectives, sectors involved, kinds of relationships among partners, location of partners, size and number of partners, targeted region, and time-horizon of the alliance.

Table 3.1 shows the different kinds of export consortia, classified according to a number of factors. Objectives and scope are perhaps the most widely adopted classification criteria as they differentiate between promotional and sales consortia, which represent the two main types of consortia.

Basically, promotional consortia are created to promote the products of their partners, but do not engage in sales activity. For this reason, they are less complex than sales consortia, where the objective of the alliance is actually to sell the partner firms' products in foreign markets. Promotional consortia invest most of their financial and human resources in marketing, whereas sales consortia act as a distribution channel for the partners, and therefore require greater investment in order to set up a sales organization.

Table 3.1 Classifications of export consortia according to different factors

Factor	Different kinds of consortia
Scope and objectives	Promotional *vs* sales consortia
Sectors involved	Single-sector *vs* multi-sector consortia
Relationships among partners	Consortia of competitors *vs* non-competitors
Location of partners	Regional *vs* multiregional consortia
	Domestic *vs* International consortia
Size and number of partners	Simple *vs* complex consortia
Targeted region	Consortia targeting a specific region *vs* acting on a global scale
Time-horizon	Short-term *vs* long-term consortia
Ownership structure	Private *vs* public consortia

Table 3.2 The strategic characteristics of sales consortia and promotional consortia

	Sales consortia	Promotional consortia
Firms' commitment to the domestic market	High	Low or absent
Firms' commitment to cooperate in foreign markets	High	High
Areas for exploitation of economies of scale	Various	Various
Coordination costs	High	Low
Involvement of individual entrepreneurs	High	Medium-low
Need for common quality standards among partners	High	Low

Table 3.2 illustrates the main strategic characteristics of both sales and promotional consortia. A comparison of the two reveals a number of significant differences that affect how they are managed.

The first important difference between the two kinds of consortium concerns the *different commitment of partners when targeting domestic or foreign markets*. Usually, the partners in an export sales consortium may also be strongly committed to cooperating with each other in the domestic market, whereas promotional consortia are often set up by firms that compete with each other at the domestic level and only wish to cooperate in exploring new foreign markets. Consequently, promotional consortia invest much less in the development of personal and social relationships among partners than sales consortia, where the pursuit of a common goal is much stronger.

Differences between export sales and promotional consortia lie also in the *types of economies of scale they can exploit*. Sales consortia can exploit economies of scale in terms of distribution channels, sales force and brand names, whereas promotional consortia usually only benefit through sharing costs (fares and other travelling expenses), due to the narrow range of business activities shared by member firms. As a result, the potential for exploiting economies of scale is much smaller in promotional consortia. This explains the greater commitment of sales consortia to cooperation. For the same reason, *coordination costs* are generally much higher than those of promotional consortia.

The *need for common quality standards* is generally low in promotional consortia. When the objective is promotion, firms can easily cooperate even if their competitive positioning is different in terms of quality. This is the case, for example, when a large number of firms, from different industries and with different strategies, share the cost of visiting a foreign country to meet different customers or distribution agents. Common quality standards, however, are a key factor in sales consortia, as the partners are expected to aim their products (whether complementary or competing) at the same customers. A common quality standard becomes even more important if they decide to share a brand name and wish to invest in developing a specific consortium image.

As a result of the many differences discussed above, sales and promotional consortia face different managerial and market problems. Sales consortia may suffer from: an incomplete or heterogeneous range of products; a lack of sales competences; problems related to the skills and behaviour of the sales manager; insufficient quality of the products of one or more partners, which has a negative impact on the image of the other partners; inappropriate prices charged by one or more of the firms, which negatively affect the value proposition of the consortium. On the other hand, promotional consortia may face difficulties due to: an inconsistent image among partners and differences in product quality and pricing which prevent the promotion of the consortium as a whole; insufficient resources invested in consortium activities; differences in the interests and objectives of the partners in terms of geographical markets and target market segments.

The higher the number of partners, the more difficult it can be to identify a shared objective and manage the group (Barney and Griffin 1992), and the greater the differences between partners (mainly from a cultural point of view), the more complex it is to coordinate their activities within the consortium. Moreover, the less balanced the power of the partners, the more difficult it can be to avoid conflict: equal contributions from all partners are considered to be one of the critical factors for a successful alliance (Hoffman and Schlosser 2001). As Ghauri et al. (2003) point out, there is no agreement on the key success factors of interfirm networks. Research results underline the fact that trust and learning processes are crucial, but the development of effective networks is possible even if the entrepreneurs have had no previous relationships with each other.

The main weakness of export consortia compared to other forms of cooperation lies in the loose ties among member firms. As the start-up of an export consortium does not require major investments, there is a risk that the partners may not put in as much effort as they should when the results are lower than originally planned. Problems arise therefore because their strategic commitment is relatively limited. This is not the case with other types of cooperative agreements, such as joint ventures which, on the contrary, require much greater financial and organizational involvement. Table 3.3 compares export consortia with other modes of entering foreign markets, namely joint ventures, and foreign direct investments (FDIs).

Considering the strengths and weaknesses of consortia in relation to other entry modes, we note that their strengths are well aligned with the typical weaknesses of SMEs, which often have insufficient financial and human resources to participate in joint ventures effectively.

Table 3.3 Export consortia and other foreign market entry modes

	Export consortia	
	Strengths	Weaknesses
Compared to **"Direct/indirect exports"**	Shared financial resources	Less focus on what is relevant to the individual firm
	Access to partners' skills and know-how	Limited strategic autonomy of firms
	Risk sharing	Need to negotiate and 'compromise' with partners
	Exploitation of economies of scale (e.g. in advertising and promotional activities)	
	Greater bargaining power	
	Possibility to offer a full range of products	
Compared to **"Foreign direct investments"**	Less investment	Less focus on what is relevant to the individual firm
	Lower risk	Limited strategic autonomy of firms
		Need to negotiate and 'compromise' with partners
Compared to **"Joint ventures"**	Less investment	Lower commitment by partners
	Lower risk	
	Fewer constraints (in terms of strategic autonomy)	

Consortia give their member firms greater bargaining power when negotiating with international customers and suppliers, and enable them to share risks. On the other hand, even when they operate in a single sector, sometimes they are not sufficiently focused on the specific objectives of each individual partner.

3.3 Export Consortia from a Dynamic Perspective: The Lifecycle of the Firm-Consortium Relationship

Export consortia are networks of firms that can last for long periods of time, though not necessarily with the same partners. Observation of export consortia shows that, although they are started up by a particular set of partners, they usually evolve over time. In very few cases do all the partners stay in the consortium (growing as the consortium grows) for the whole of the consortium's life. In most cases, some partners leave while other new partners join at various stages of the network's life-cycle.

Although, at first glance, a firm's departure could be seen as a failure on the part of the consortium, this is not always strictly true. Firms change over time, and so do their needs: this is normal. For example, after a certain period, a member firm may have developed such a strong internationalization strategy that it no longer feels the need to be part of the consortium. On other occasions, firms also leave when they

3.3 Export Consortia from a Dynamic Perspective

realize they are too different from the other partners. This is a fairly frequent problem among export consortia. It usually occurs when most consortium members are very small and one member is medium-sized or when the reverse is true: when the majority are medium-sized and only one is small. In the latter case – which is more common – it often happens that the small firm cannot afford those investments which appear reasonable to the other members. And the end result is usually that the small firm leaves the network.

The framework proposed by Renart (2002) about the lifecycle of a firm's involvement in an export consortium is a useful tool to better understand and manage the dynamics of change that affect the relationship between the firms and the network and, ultimately, the end of the consortium.

Building on his empirical observation of Spanish export consortia, Renart (2002) maintains that, in Spain, most export consortia are estimated to have a total life cycle of between 6 and 10 years, the first 2 years being dedicated to the consortium's gestation and the rest to effective operations. In Spain, it is common practice for member firms to use the consortium as an 'export launch ramp', that is, as a time-limited subsidized cooperation mechanism. This mechanism is dissolved or abandoned as soon as the firms perceive that they have established a strategic platform which allows them to continue exporting independently.

Figure 3.1 illustrates how the involvement of a member firm can change over time. The framework assumes that a firm's decision whether or not to join the consortium basically depends (over time) on the difference between the total benefits it perceives from belonging to the consortium (Total Motivation to Belong, TMB) and the value of advantages that at any given moment the firm attributes to other alternative modes of internationalization (Total Motivation to Alternatives, TMAs). At any moment the TMB to a consortium is equal to the differences between *advantages and the costs of participation*. Both advantages and costs

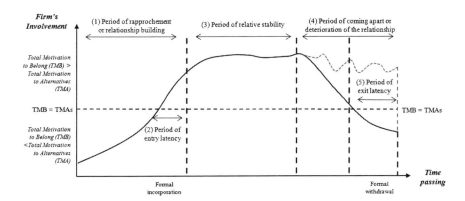

Fig. 3.1 The lifecycle of a firm's involvement in an export consortium (*Source*: Adapted from Renart 2002)

need to be understood in their broad sense, i.e., not only economic costs and advantages. Alternatives to participating in a consortium may be represented, for example, by the autonomous internationalization that firms can achieve by hiring an export manager or setting up a joint venture with a foreign partner. TMAs therefore represent the highest among alternative motivations when there is more than one alternative. This explains why consortia are unstable networks and why it is so important that a consortium partner has the perception of receiving from the consortium benefits that are higher than the costs and disadvantages associated with participation, as well as compared to other alternatives for internationalization.

The basic idea behind Renart's model is that *the motivation to belong* to a consortium is the key variable in explaining why a member firm decides to enter, stay, or leave a consortium.

At the very beginning the TMB is either totally absent or very low. Its gradual increase characterizes the initial stage of rapprochement or building a relationship (1) with the consortium. When TMB finally exceeds TMAs, the firm decides on formal incorporation, usually after an initial period of entry latency (2). Once it has joined consortium, the firm experiences day to day the advantages of being a part of the network and, if all goes well, a period of relative stability (3) follows. As the dotted line shows, the high level of satisfaction of a firm (with a very high TMB) may last for a long period if there is a strategic alignment among member firms and the consortium provides effective results for all. Sometimes, however, events produce a different scenario: this happens when the firm begins to come apart or when there is a deterioration in the relationships within the consortium (4). At this point, for the firm, TMB begins to appear less appealing than other alternatives (TMAs). This may cause the firm to head gradually towards final withdrawal from the consortium, possibly preceded by a period of exit latency (5).

Therefore, the decision to be part of the consortium is always continuously assessed by the entrepreneurs. The balance between benefits/costs and the perception of benefits and costs are the most significant issues for the development and stability of consortia. This must also be an important concern for a consortium's management team as well as for the network facilitator.

3.4 The Diffusion of Export Consortia in Developed Countries

Despite the fact that participation in export consortia can bring many benefits to SMEs, export consortia are not very widespread globally and it is difficult to obtain relevant data. In this section we attempt to illustrate how export consortia are distributed.

As far as Europe is concerned, export consortia seem to be mainly concentrated in the southern part of the continent. Indeed, they are fairly widespread in Italy and Spain, where they have been popular for many years. Both Italy and Spain are considered pioneers in the field. Export consortia also exist in Portugal and France, but they are not popular in other European countries (such as the United Kingdom

3.4 The Diffusion of Export Consortia in Developed Countries   53

and Germany) where there is an abundance of R&D and purchasing consortia, but no substantial evidence for the existence of export consortia.

The diffusion of export consortia depends on the presence of public policies or institutions promoting and supporting them and often they are also protected by national associations or organizations which represent their interest at the political level.

In Italy, for instance, many export consortia are associated with *Federexport*, which is the association of export consortia within *Confindustria*, the leading business association in the country. According to the 2008 Report on export consortia activities (Federexport 2009), there are around 120 export consortia associated with Federexport, with a total number of 3,778 member firms. The number of export consortia has not increased in recent years, but the number of firms has. Over the last few years there have been no financial measures or specific programmes to support the creation and development of new export consortia, as there were in the past. This is one of the main reasons why Italy has a long history of cooperation in the form of export consortia. Sometimes export consortia in Italy also develop without the support of public administration, as they are traditionally seen as an effective way of overcoming weaknesses deriving from the small size of firms.

In Spain, a national programme of the Spanish Institute for Export (ICEX – Instituto Español de Comercio Exterior) favoured the creation of 95 export consortia in the period 1985–1992. Up to 2000, the total number of consortia supported by ICEX was 330. Subsequently, another 60–70 consortia were supported during the 2001–2004 period (ICEX 2005). The same programme was still in operation in 2008, providing financial support aimed at the creation of export consortia or associations of new exporters.

In France there are also measures in place to support the international development of small enterprises if they are artisans. These measures are related to the certification procedure to obtain a specific label and, in some cases, lead to the development of consortia.

On the basis of the experience of export consortia in Southern Europe, we can summarize the main factors for the success of cooperation as follows:

- the *very small size of firms in these countries* and the subsequent lack of resources and other weaknesses associated with small size, which may be overcome through participation in export consortia;
- a strong, general and increasing *orientation towards export* of the national economies of the countries, particularly in the manufacturing industries, also because of the integration of the European market;
- the presence of *specific supporting programmes* adopted and financed by local and national governments or local chambers of commerce;
- the existence of *specific laws establishing special advantages* for firms when aggregating in the consortium mode.

It is not easy to find similar experiences outside Europe. In the USA, for example, consortia are mainly formed in the education sector or are oriented towards R&D activities. American firms tend to go international through direct export or foreign direct investments rather than through interfirm collaborations. This is consistent with the fact that US firms have a more individualistic approach to business. Moreover, as firms have a large domestic market, they are not motivated to become international if they do not believe they have the pre-requisites to do so successfully (as may be the case for smaller firms). Conversely, in most European countries, domestic markets are too small for the survival and development of firms. This forces them to search for sales opportunities abroad and rely on cooperation to achieve the goal of moving onto the international market.

3.5 Export Consortia in Developing Countries

Firms from developing and emerging countries are often small, lack financial resources, and do not have specific international competences, experience and knowledge of foreign markets. Participating in a consortium may therefore be a means of starting the internationalization process and acquiring the skills and know-how necessary to operate successfully abroad. As consortia foster learning and the acquisition of internationalization competences, the number of consortia can be expected to increase.

There is little data concerning the diffusion of consortia in developing countries, but they seem to be relatively rare. This is true not only for export consortia, but also for other types of consortia.

In Argentina, due to the combined effect of a specific law plus support programmes, export consortia have existed since the 1980s. In 2008, according to UNIDO (2008), there were at least 55 export consortia, which is a relatively high number compared to other countries from the same area.

According to Scherer et al. (2009), for example, consortia are not unusual in the heavy construction industry in Brazil, though they are not export-oriented. Some export consortia do exist, supported mainly by APEX – Brazil (Trade and Investment promotion agency). As shown in a report by Rodrigues Silva (2005), 70 export consortia were created with the support of APEX – Brazil in the period 1998–2005. In 2005, the same agency supported the creation of 13 export consortia.

There are also several export consortia in other Latin American countries, though they are neither very numerous nor particulary active. For Peru, the export of goods is a strategic priority, and this explains the existence of at least 30 export consortia which are considered crucial for the international growth of SMEs (Lima Chamber of Commerce 2005). Uruguay represents a similar situation; (Saegaert 2005) where the role of cooperation aimed at the development of exports is recognized, even though no specific corporate designation exists for consortia.

In East European countries and some Middle Eastern countries, export consortia have not developed at all. In 2005, for example, there were no export consortia in Croatia (Mesic 2005) Romania (Ionescu and Bratu 2005) or Lebanon (Oueini and Ladki 2005), all of which are countries where there are many small firms which could benefit from the possibility of cooperation in the form of consortia. Exceptions to this include Turkey where, in 2005, the existence of 30 export consortia was reported as a result of support programmes implemented by different bodies (Kunt 2005) and Jordan, where there are three consortia, which formed following several years of UNIDO support (Al-Hindawi 2007).

Export consortia are relatively well-developed in some North African countries, such as Tunisia and Morocco. There are at least 20 export consortia in Tunisia and, including those in the development phase, more than 30 in Morocco. In both cases the consortia have benefited from support programmes where UNIDO was a key player in the development of these export networks. Some are included in our empirical analysis and described in detail in Chap. 4.

3.6 The Experience of the United Nations Industrial Development Organization in Promoting SME Export Consortia

Creating the conditions for consortia development is a demanding task. Owing to a lack of knowledge and weak institutional and regulatory frameworks, attempts to establish export groups of SMEs in developing countries often fail. As a result, external assistance may be critical for developing a sound export consortia programme.

Capitalizing on its long experience in SME cluster and network development, in 2005 UNIDO developed a comprehensive programme to assist developing countries and transition economies in establishing export consortia. The various initiatives of UNIDO in the field of SME network development, including export consortia, are ongoing in many countries. These include Ecuador, Colombia, Peru, Uruguay, Nicaragua, Morocco, Tunisia, Senegal, Nigeria, Ethiopia, Jordan, The Lebanon, Iran, Pakistan and India. Despite the recentness of the UNIDO export consortia programme, it has already given rise to a wide range of initiatives around the world.

In Morocco, since 2004, UNIDO has supported the Moroccan Ministry of Foreign Trade and the Moroccan Exporters Association (ASMEX) in setting up an export consortia development programme in the country. As a result, 20 export consortia have been legally formalized so far and 11 are under development. In 2009, 156 SMEs were actively involved in the project, accounting for more than 15,800 jobs across 11 industries in as many cities.

In Tunisia, in a matter of just a few years, UNIDO has promoted 20 export consortia in the sectors of engineering and consulting, processed food, car components, textile-garment, furniture and ICT. The intervention of UNIDO – in partnership with the Ministry of Industry, FAMEX (World Bank) and CEPEX (Export Promotion Agency) – has contributed to the introduction of a new culture of networking among small businesses.

In 2006, in response to a request from the Peruvian authorities, UNIDO set up a project in Peru with the objective of tackling the problems faced by SMEs when trying to export. The results of this project are 30 export consortia, created in eight different regions of Peru representing a wide range of industries including jewellery, information technologies and tourism, textiles and garment-making, processed food, metal-mechanics, ICT, natural products, furniture, tourism and ceramics.

UNIDO's assistance in promoting export consortia in developing countries focuses on:

- *Supporting the creation of export consortia.* Groups of SMEs are identified and coached throughout the process of consortium development: identification of common objectives and consortium services to be provided, choice of corporate designation, development of the business plan and implementation of pilot promotional activities. UNIDO support is temporary and therefore includes the identification of technical and financial programmes that can support the development of export consortia in the long term, and assistance in preparing firms' requests for access to these programmes.
- *Capacity building for public institutions that promote or regulate export consortia.* This includes workshops and study tours, introducing the concept to policy-makers, improving legislative and policy frameworks and developing an incentive system.
- *Capacity building for private sector institutions that provide assistance for the establishment and operation of export consortia.* Organizations such as business associations, chambers of commerce, regional agencies and export consultants are made aware of the benefits of consortia and learn how to support their establishment and operation through training, presentations by experts, study tours and benchmarking exercises.
- *Skills development for export consortium managers.* This activity includes the provision of information, workshops, discussion forums, best practice demonstrations, meetings with consortium promoters and demonstration projects showing how consortium participants can overcome misgivings and undertake cooperative projects.

Since the start of its programme in developing countries, UNIDO has established a strategic alliance with Federexport (the Italian Federation of Export Consortia) and ICEX (the Spanish Institute for Foreign Trade) in order to strengthen the learning opportunities deriving from the two countries with the greatest expertise among developed economies in the field of export consortia.

In addition to country-specific support, UNIDO offers global and regional training courses (including distance learning) and organizes study tours and expert group meetings to disseminate good practices. Through the organization of such events, UNIDO makes its expertise available to public and private institutions around the world and shares the benefits of its experience in export consortia development.[1]

In constructing a picture of export consortia throughout the world, we have to recognize that UNIDO, since 2010, has been the main contributor to the

---

[1] Additional information is available at www.unido.org/exportconsortia.

Table 3.4 Export consortia supported by UNIDO in 2010

Countries	No. of export consortia supported by UNIDO
Jordan	3
Morocco	20 + 11 under development
Peru	30
Senegal	3
Tunisia	20
Uruguay	3
Total	90

Source: UNIDO (www.unido.org)

development of export consortia in developing countries in partnership with local authorities and bodies. Table 3.4 illustrates how many export consortia are supported by UNIDO and their location: they number around 90. If we consider five to be the average number of firms belonging to any given export consortium, we can estimate that around 450 firms are involved in UNIDO programmes.

The cooperation between UNIDO and local institutions, such as governments, export associations and chambers of commerce, is an important factor for success, as different kinds of support are necessary for the international development of SMEs and each of the institutions mentioned can supply one or more types of support. These include money, contracts, business contacts and managerial assistance.

In such a context, UNIDO (through its officers and consultants) plays the role of network facilitator, as defined in Chap. 2: it promotes the partnership among the firms, but also builds the relationships with the other national stakeholders (including public institutions) and promotes the collection of tangible and intangible resources for developing the consortium.

References

Al-Hindawi, A. (2007). Country paper Jordan. UNIDO, www.unido.org
Barney, J., & Griffin, R. W. (1992). *The management of organizations: Strategy, structure, behavior*. Boston: Houghton Mifflin.
Berrada, A. (2007). Country paper Morocco, www.unido.org
Depperu, D. (1996). *Economia dei consorzi tra imprese*. Milano: Egea.
Federexport. (2009). *Rapporto Federexport 2008*, Rome.
Ghauri, P., Lutz, C., & Tedfom, G. (2003). Using networks to solve export-marketing problems of small- and medium-sized firms from developing countries. *European Journal of Marketing, 37*(5/6), 728–752.
Hoffman, W. H., & Schlosser, R. (2001). Success factors of strategic alliances in small and medium-sized enterprises – An empirical survey. *Long Range Planning, 34*(3), 357–381.
ICEX. (2005). Export consortia, www.unido.org
Ionescu, S., & Bratu, R. (2005). Country paper Romania, UNIDO, www.unido.org
Kunt, V. (2005). Country paper Turkey. UNIDO, www.unido.org
Lima Chamber of Commerce. (2005). Country paper Peru. www.unido.org
Mesic, Z. (2005). Country paper Croatia. UNIDO, www.unido.org
Oueini, S. S., & Ladki, N. (2005). Country paper Lebanon, www.unido.org

Renart, L. G. (2002). *The cycle of a single company's involvement in an export consortium*, Research Paper n. 477, October, IESE.
Rodrigues Silva, A. (2005). Country paper Brazil. UNIDO, www.unido.org
Saegaert, J. (2005). Country paper Uruguay. UNIDO, www.unido.org
Scherer, F. L., Gomes, C. M., & Kruglianskas, I. (2009). The internationalization process of Brazilian companies: A study of multiple cases in the heavy construction industry. *Brazilian Administrative Review, 6*(4), 280–298.
UNIDO. (2003). *Development of clusters and networks of SMEs: The UNIDO programme. A guide to export consortia*, Wien.
UNIDO. (2008). *Relevamiento (Mapeo) De La Situación De Los Consorcios De Exportación En La República Argentina*. www.unido.org
Welch, D. E., Welch, L. S., Young, L. C., & Wilkinson, I. F. (1998). The importance of networks in export promotion: Policy issues. *Journal of International Marketing, 6*(4), 66–82.

4 Empirical Analysis of Nine Export Consortia of SMEs in Morocco, Tunisia, Peru and Uruguay

4.1 The Field Research: Data Collection and Analysis

In this chapter we present the empirical evidence on which our work builds. Such evidence is based on the analysis of nine export consortia promoted by the United Nations Industrial Development Organization (UNIDO) in developing countries between 2004 and 2007: four in Peru, three in Morocco, and one each in Tunisia and Uruguay. These consortia all promote the products of their member firms in international markets, succeeding in enhancing the international competitiveness of tens of local micro and small firms.

At the beginning of 2008, UNIDO staff in Vienna asked ALTIS (Postgraduate School of Business and Society at the Università Cattolica del Sacro Cuore in Milan, Italy) to study the experience of the export consortia promoted by the UNIDO programme. We were therefore offered the opportunity to collaborate with local UNIDO officers in developing countries, in order to study in depth the business models and performance of some export consortia established in different countries.

The primary aim of the research was to analyze how these networks have designed and put into practice their strategies in terms of objectives, initiatives and selection of target markets. In addition, the empirical analysis covered the organizational model and systems of corporate governance that export consortia have adopted and the goals achieved by both the consortium as a whole and the individual member firms. Our objective was to test the validity of the UNIDO model and develop a general framework for the strategic management of export consortia.

Although the relevance of export consortia for the international competitiveness of small firms in both industrialized and developing countries is largely acknowledged, there has so far been little academic interest in this professional practice and export consortia remain almost completely neglected in the pages of mainstream journals and other academic publications. Export consortia appear to represent one example of an area of professional practice that management research has not been able to analyze, or shown sufficient interest in doing so, despite its economic relevance and social implications (Pfeffer 2009).

In order to carry out an in-depth analysis of the export consortia, a case-study approach was adopted (Eisenhardt 1989; Yin 1989), consistent with previous research on the internationalization of SMEs from a network perspective (Chetty and Holm 2000). A case study investigates a contemporary phenomenon within its own context (Yin 1989). The selection of nine cases was made in accordance with Eisenhardt (1989) who, while stating that in the multiple-case approach there is no ideal number of cases, recommends between four and ten.

The export consortia to be analyzed were selected on the basis of three criteria: (a) age, focusing on the oldest among a panel composed entirely of relatively recently established consortia, in order to have a significant time-frame to analyze; (b) evidence of success in business, in order to identify best practices; (c) operation in different sectors, so as to provide examples of the application of these network models to different industrial contexts in developing countries.

The field research was carried out between April and October 2008 and involved nine consortia, whose names and profiles are shown in Table 4.1. During our work, a set of research tools was developed to collect and organize qualitative and quantitative information about the cases.

The data for analysis were collected by means of interviews with the consortia managers and entrepreneurs, and cover two levels of analysis:
(a) Export consortium;
(b) Member firms.

Given this double level of analysis, two different questionnaires were initially developed and discussed with officers and field managers from UNIDO and then tested. A pilot test on a small group of entrepreneurs and managers enabled us to refine our research tools.

The two questionnaires were then submitted to the target consortia. The first questionnaire was submitted to the general manager of each consortium and designed to collect data concerning:
- *characteristics and history* of the consortium: year of incorporation, number and size of member firms, legal form and organizational structure, operational and promotional costs;
- *funding and members' contributions*;
- *objectives and strategies*: target markets, marketing and promotional activities, initiatives and services and their evolution over time;
- *relationships between the consortium and its members*;
- *performance,* in terms of the opening of new markets for member firms and increasing export sales.

The second questionnaire was submitted to the individual entrepreneurs, enabling us to collect information about the member firms. In particular, the interviews shed light on the firms' activities and organization (including international experience and competences, type and amount of foreign activities, characteristics of export staff – if any), and changes in the firm's activities as a result of its consortium membership.

4.1 The Field Research: Data Collection and Analysis 61

Table 4.1 Consortia profiles

#	Country	Consortium	Year of foundation	Type of consortium	Member firms	Size of firms	Industry
1.	Morocco	**Mosaic**	2004	Promotional	6 privately owned firms	Medium-large (120–330 employees)	Textiles and garments
2.	Morocco	**Vitargan**	2005	Promotional	6 cooperatives	Small and medium (17–69 employees)	Agribusiness (oil of argan)
3.	Morocco	**Travel Partners**	2006	Promotional	7 travel agencies	Micro-small (5–23 employees)	Tourist services
4.	Tunisia	**Get'IT**	2005	Promotional	11 providers of ICT and Web solutions	Mainly medium-sized enterprises (5–100 employees)	Information and communication technologies
5.	Peru	**Muyu**	2005	Promotional	5 artisan firms	Micro-small (5–20 employees)	Traditional handicrafts
6.	Peru	**Peruvian Bio Consortia**	2006	Promotional	3 family firms	Small (21–37 employees)	Agribusiness (plant extracts, nutritional and cosmetic products)
7.	Peru	**ACMC**	2007	Sales	4 integrated manufacturers	Small (35–53 employees)	Metal furnishings (production and machinery)
8.	Peru	**Ande Natura**	2007	Promotional	5 family firms	Micro-small (5–20 employees)	Agribusiness (herbs and organic food)
9.	Uruguay	**Phyto Uruguay**	2005	Sales	9 family firms	Micro-small (5–27 employees)	Herbal and nutraceutical

Nine detailed reports on each consortium and its member firms were developed in accordance with a common framework. These final reports have been the basis for the brief case histories presented in this chapter and for the development of the framework for analyzing the strategic management of export consortia presented in Chapter 5.

4.2   Mosaic (Morocco)

The promotional consortium Mosaic in Casablanca was instituted in 2004 and represents the first export consortium to be created in Morocco. Compared to other consortia, it may appear rather anomalous due to the characteristics of its members – six relatively large textile and garment manufacturers. All are proud of their previous export experience. Firm 'A' (330 employees) produces underwear and corsetry; Firm 'B' (195 employees), shirts and nightwear; Firm 'C' (140 employees), sweaters and knitwear; Firm 'D' (220 employees), pyjamas and children's wear; Firm 'E' (120 employees), knitwear; and finally Firm 'F' (230 employees) produces parkas, anoraks and professional clothing. When the consortium was created, all these firms were already producing as subcontractors for large international retailers, almost exclusively for foreign markets, mainly France, Britain and Spain, but also Italy, Ireland and Belgium. However, they were all seeking ways to raise their international competitiveness and add value to their final products.

The firms are very homogeneous in terms of size, sector and international competences, but also highly complementary in terms of customers and products. This is a very favourable condition for developing shared consortium strategies as the profiles and interests of the members are substantially aligned.

The original group which launched the consortium in 2004 was less homogeneous, as it included other small firms. However, these firms soon realized that they would be unable to follow the ambitious action plan supported by the larger firms and so left the consortium. They have been replaced by larger and more experienced members.

Given the international experience of its members, the consortium's activities are subordinated to the autonomous strategic patterns of the individual firms. They do not consider the consortium as the main tool for their internationalization but as a means of
- *fostering their individual competitive advantages* in their markets, by improving their managerial competences and increasing their strategic resources;
- *further developing exports*;
- *extending and diversifying their trading opportunities*, by means of new subcontracting and co-contracting activities.

Mosaic has identified three strategic objectives: to improve the competitiveness of its members; to promote and develop its members' exports, and diversify their trading opportunities; and to develop its members' ability to propose creative finished products.

4.2 Mosaic (Morocco)

The efforts and investments of the consortium are therefore oriented simultaneously in two directions:
- *Downstream*: Mosaic creates brand communications and marketing initiatives aimed at new prospects for its collective portfolio of products. The advantage for firms cooperating derive from sharing the costs of producing promotional tools, participating in international trade fairs and organizing trade missions abroad.
- *Upstream*: the consortium manages collective projects for the development of the internal processes and systems of the individual firms. Examples of these projects include: staff training in design, style and manufacturing processes, restructuring offices and departments, installing strategic information systems, guiding cost reduction programmes and collectively negotiating better conditions from suppliers of goods and services. In this case, the additional advantage of the consortium for the individual members lies in economies of scale, quicker and easier access to new external competences, and collective access to public funds.

The organizational structure of Mosaic is very 'light': the consortium does not have its own premises or dedicated offices, but rather relies on the physical and managerial resources of its members. Nevertheless, a more binding and demanding stage in the consortium's life cycle is on the horizon, and will probably affect both its strategy and business model.

The governance system is also very simple. All six members are involved in everyday management and hold a formal half-day meeting once a month. Through frequent interaction, they strengthen the transfer of knowledge and the consortium is therefore a low-cost means of improving the capabilities of the member firms. The mutual coaching of managers has been established by identifying branches, dividing tasks and organizing regular meetings. This has allowed the companies to take advantage of the group's internal expertise without bearing the cost of hiring specific experts to fill organizational gaps.

The owner behind the largest firm has been appointed president of the consortium. He is also responsible for the branch of the Moroccan Association for Textile and Garment Industries (AMITH) which promotes and supports export consortia. This link strengthens the relationship between Mosaic and AMITH.

The issue of guaranteeing each member a fair and satisfactory balance between commitment (in terms of financial and human contributions) and benefits has been solved by means of a flexible and highly pragmatic mechanism. The consortium has embraced a kind of 'variable geometry' paradigm, based on the idea that not every firm needs to take part in every activity, and some may cooperate more closely on different projects. The programme of activities is therefore decided by the firms on the basis of their main targets, and any members who are not interested in one specific action do not participate in it. Consequently, the consortium does not ask for a fixed annual contribution from its members. Rather, each activity is equally financed by the participants, who usually also benefit from public co-financing for the specific project.

According to the entrepreneurs, after four years of activity, the main results achieved by Mosaic are: the restructuring of the member firms; better positioning on the international market and the establishment of an efficient and effective system of competitive intelligence. In particular, members' perceptions of consortium objectives indicate that the strategic goal of improving the competitiveness of the individual firms in their traditional markets has been more successfully achieved than others. There is still much left to do in order to promote and develop members' exports, diversify their trade opportunities and direct members towards more competitive finished products.

The member firms consider their competences to have improved, particularly in terms of technical expertise and their ability to analyze international markets, and that their relational capital has also increased in terms of business contacts abroad. However, the main perceived benefit has been identified as a better corporate image in the eyes of both customers and suppliers.

4.3 Vitargan (Morocco)

Vitargan was set up in 2005 by six cooperatives of argan oil producers in the region of Essaouira, Morocco. They produce oil that is both for cosmetic use and food-grade. The consortium was created within the framework of a broader project financed by the European Union (in partnership with local economic development agencies). The aim of this project was to encourage the production of argan oil in the area between Essaouira and Agadir provinces and promote the role of women in rural areas and their contribution to economic and social development.

The six SMEs involved in the consortium have different degrees of experience in foreign markets. Firm 'A' (69 employees) exports 80% of its production to France. Also for Firm 'B' (54 employees) exports account for 80% of its sales, mainly to France and Italy. Firm 'C' (21 employees), Firm 'D' (60 employees) and Firm 'E' (60 employees) export only 10% of their production, mainly to France, Germany, Italy and Switzerland. Finally Firm 'F', the smallest firm in the group (with only 17 employees), has no export activity.

The argan oil producers formed the consortium to achieve the following strategic objectives: (1) To increase the production of cosmetic-grade and food-grade argan oil; (2) to promote high quality biological production; (3) to share purchases of raw materials, machinery and other sourcing activities; (4) to improve product marketing and (5) to develop a common image.

Originally, the goal of their alliance was to reduce purchasing and service costs, but the member firms soon decided to develop a joint packaging process and shared promotion, communication and marketing campaigns. Currently, each cooperative firm owns its machinery but they are now considering the opportunity to centralize the refinement phase of the oil by giving it directly to the consortium. The cooperatives would sell the oil to the consortium, which would then be responsible for refining and marketing it. The member firms are also aligning their image and communication strategies under the consortium banner by creating leaflets and a website to promote the cooperatives.

Training is very important for Vitargan. Various courses have been organized for the member firms, focusing on the valorization of argan oil and its products, the best production practices and international marketing. These activities have given rise to a kind of production handbook, forming the basis for the international certification (ECOCERT) of argan oil.

The organizational structure of the consortium resembles that of its member firms. It has a president (on a two-year appointment), vice-president, board of directors (the members of which are the presidents of the six cooperatives), treasurer, vice-treasurer, secretary and vice-secretary. It also has an external managing director, remunerated directly by the members. Regular meetings are held at members' offices on a monthly or weekly basis, as required.

All of the firms contribute to covering 25% of the operating costs from their own resources, while the remaining 75% (including promotional and product packaging/refinement costs) is covered by the Argan Project, financed by the European Union. All the main activities of the consortium are co-financed by public institutions.

During 2006, the consortium developed a common identity and communication system, which significantly enhanced marketing and communication effectiveness, and has allowed the cooperatives to participate in a number of national and international trade fairs and exhibitions. In order to participate in these events (e.g. the SIAL exhibition, a fair in Montreaux, and the ANUGA in Cologne) they produced common leaflets and a collective website. Alongside these activities, Vitargan also promotes initiatives in favour of female workers and the literacy of women in the region, and has supported the role of women by creating a new family code (*Moudawana*).

The marketing and commercial strategies of the consortium are identified by the managing director and approved by the board. However, although the members have developed a slightly greater mutual confidence and openness two years on from the establishment of the consortium, they are still reluctant to delegate decision-making powers to the managing director. Consequently, decisions are taken by the board of directors. This has raised concerns on the part of the managing director about the slowness of the decision-making process, which results in delays in the definition of action plans, as well as the planning and organization of national and international trade missions.

The creation of Vitargan has allowed member firms to obtain substantial results. Firstly, cost-sharing and cost-reduction have been achieved by means of centralized purchases and the use of joint conditioning. This has also led to an increase in production capacity. Secondly, the firms have obtained the ECOCERT BIO quality certification, which increases the value of the product for their customers. Thirdly, participation in the most important international trade fairs and exhibitions has provided significant opportunities for firms to meet potential partners, customers and competitors in the global market. The consortium decided to focus its marketing activities primarily on the German, Italian, Spanish, French, Canadian and US markets. Fourthly, an important result is the firms' increase in quality control procedures – in this regard the consortium is considered by its member firms to have fully achieved the objective of valorizing the quality of their product. Finally, partners are also satisfied with the development of a common image, even though they acknowledge that improvement is still needed in terms of marketing.

Some further important considerations about the consortium's achievements arise from the results of the survey of the cooperatives. The entrepreneurs acknowledge that their marketing capabilities and knowledge of foreign markets have both improved since they joined the consortium. They agree that the image of their firms has improved significantly in the eyes of both customers and suppliers. However, the number of foreign customers and business contacts has increased only slightly. The need for a more structured organization to enhance the process of export development is still perceived as a gap to be filled.

4.4 Travel Partners (Morocco)

Travel Partners Morocco (TPM) is the first export consortium created in Morocco within the service sector. It was officially founded in 2006, with the support of the UNIDO-Foreign Trade Ministry project. It is officially defined as a Group of Economic Interest and comprises seven competing travel agencies in the Casablanca area, which offer similar services and have the same market positioning. All the firms are small in size, ranging from 5 to 23 employees.

The firms decided to form the consortium in order to strengthen the promotion of Morocco abroad and position themselves among the leaders of the travel agency sector at a national level. They are now the third largest player in terms of turnover in the Moroccan market. In addition to the objective mentioned above, the member firms also wanted to improve their negotiating and purchasing power, establish a sort of benchmarking system and develop knowledge-sharing routines. Regarding international competitive strategy, the consortium has decided to focus on developing its products, entering new foreign markets and creating an image of travel agencies according to certain principles and ethical values.

Marketing strategies and trade missions are planned by common agreement, focusing on the most strategic target countries (such as the UK, Germany, France, Spain, the USA and Russia) and the opportunity to enter new and untapped niche markets (such as 'golf tourism').

The consortium has adopted a collegiate management system in which the main tasks have been divided among four operational commissions: (a) *Purchases* from airline companies, suppliers, insurance companies, etc.: the task of this commission is not only to obtain the best purchasing conditions for the travel agencies, but also to set up a group of reliable business suppliers; (b) *Communications*: this commission coordinates all the communication and promotional activities of the consortium and its members, including a website, promotional CD-ROM and leaflets; (c) *Human resources:* the main objective is to develop a common training plan for the managers and employees of the member firms in order to boost their professionalism (the outsourcing of their HR function is envisaged for the future); (d) *Exhibitions and trade fairs:* on the basis of a joint promotion campaign, this commission is responsible for organizing the participation of members in overseas missions and meetings with foreign tour operators.

Each commission provides support services for the member firms, which see the division of tasks as one of the most important advantages of the consortium.

The consortium does not have its own premises and meetings are held in rotation at the offices of each member firm. There is an annual membership fee to cover the consortium's operating costs and each firm participating in a particular activity pays a further fee to cover that specific cost.

Since its establishment, the consortium has developed some useful communication and promotional tools for presenting the services offered by its members, such as a common catalogue and a website. Furthermore, TPM has designed a consortium logo in order to strengthen the competitive position of the firms in foreign markets. The consortium has also achieved an increase in its negotiating power, resulting in the reduction of purchasing costs and the compilation of a black list of less reliable or more expensive suppliers. In the area of human resource (HR) management the consortium is designing a system aimed at standardizing HR policies for all its members.

All the travel agency managers agree that being part of the consortium has improved their internal market positioning and provided a source of mutual information exchange which better enables them to confront new markets. In 2007, TPM hired a temporary managing director (with the job title of "coordinator") paid directly by the consortium's members. He is responsible for organizing the weekly meetings and implementing the initiatives identified in the action plan.

It is difficult to analyze the performance of the consortium within such a short period. In addition, as the firms record their own sales directly and do not attribute them to the consortium, it is difficult to evaluate the increase in revenues due specifically to the actions of the consortium.

Nevertheless, it is possible to identify three main goals achieved by the consortium:
– the development and presentation of a common image/identity;
– greater visibility on the national market;
– access to new countries and untapped niches.

The member firms are increasingly involved in a common action plan. Most of them agree that their image and competitive positioning has improved among both customers and suppliers. However, they perceive that there is a great deal still to be achieved in terms of internationalization and the development of new services.

4.5 Get'IT (Tunisia)

Get'IT is the first promotional consortium constituted in Tunisia and groups together firms belonging to the Information and Communication Technologies (ICT) sector. Officially founded in 2005, the consortium is the result of a previous one-year period of informal cooperation among six firms interested in running international activities financed by the National Fund for the Access to Export

Markets (FAMEX). This cooperation strengthened trust among the firms and encouraged them to formalize the alliance. At the beginning of 2009, the original composition of Get'IT changed and included 11 members of varying sizes, all providers of ICT services, but with little competition between them. In fact, there is no relevant overlapping of markets and, as they offer a wide range of different services, their products are fairly complementary: Firm 'A' (5 employees) is a consultancy firm specializing in webmarketing; Firm 'B'(35 employees) provides IT systems and mobility solutions; Firm 'C' (100 employees) specializes in consultancy, development and the integration of ERP and other solutions for enterprises; Firm 'D' (40 employees) offers information, web and communication solutions; Firm 'E' (20 employees) offers IT outsourcing and communication services; Firm 'F' (22 employees) offers web, multimedia and training services; Firm 'G' (20 employees), offers web-design training and development services; Firm 'H' (the largest firm, with 120 employees) offers a wide range of IT services, including management consulting; Firm 'I' (20 employees) provides IT solutions for business intelligence and decision-making processes; Firm 'J' (45 employees) provides consultancy, telecommunication, assistance and security services; and finally Firm 'K' (100 employees) manages a call centre and offers telemarketing services and hotlines. Compared to other firms in service industries in Tunisia, most of the member firms may be considered to be medium-sized.

The main strategic objectives of Get'IT are: (a) to combine members' efforts to promote the competitiveness of the network as a whole; (b) to promote Tunisia as a site for new technology outsourcing and a reliable provider of ICT services; (c) to promote the exports of member firms by means of collective action; (d) to enrich the global offer of the firms by leveraging on complementary and diversified solutions in the ICT industry.

Eighty percent of the consortium's budgetary resources are allocated to promotional activities, such as collective participation in international fairs in Europe, the organization of and participation in technical and professional conferences and forums in France and Tunisia, the organization of trade missions abroad and collective marketing activities (including the development of a common website and the creation and launch of a collective brand).

The consortium's target market during its first three years was France (which is perceived as a close market because of the common language), followed by Italy and Germany. However, members have also promoted their products in the domestic market by focusing on their ability to supply integrated solutions to local customers.

The consortium has always had a very 'light' structure, consistent with the intangible, virtual nature of its digital business. The organization and management of specific promotional activities are outsourced to an external office which provides coordinating and organizational services to Get'IT. The general management of this external office is the responsibility of a managing director, elected by the entrepreneurs. There are no professional managers, dedicated staff or management systems pertaining specifically to the consortium, only those of the individual firms. The sole exception is a common Customer Relationship Management (CRM) solution which the member firms want to implement in order to manage the consortium's main asset – the relational capital built up over three years of promotional activity and contacts.

The managing director holds office for one year, and there is no formal board of directors as all of the chief executives of the member firms participate in planning strategies and designing programmes and budgets. Moreover, possible problems are avoided owing to the consortium's highly participative governance system. Every action is discussed and directly approved in advance by the member firms in the context of intense dialogue with little or no formality.

In terms of financing, each firm provides a low fixed contribution to cover overheads, and specific activities are financed equally by the participating firms and generally co-financed by public funds.

As in the case of all promotional consortia, it is difficult to measure the impact of consortium activities on the individual firms directly. However, compared to the situation prior to the foundation of the consortium, there have been significant increases in revenues (on average +30%) and export performance. All of the firms acknowledge that they have benefited from participation in the consortium in terms of the establishment of best practices and openness to international markets.

Finally, members emphasize that the benefits obtained due to the consortium go beyond business contacts and profit. Intangible resources such as knowledge of new international markets and a better understanding of potential customers have dramatically improved.

4.6 Muyu (Peru)

Founded in 2005, the export consortium Muyu is composed of five micro and small handicraft firms based in Cusco, Peru, all of which produce handmade products associated with Peruvian tradition. More specifically, Firm 'A' (6 employees) produces garments and accessories in alpaca leather, exporting 30% of its production; Firm 'B' (12 employees) produces alpaca wool garments and sells 93% of its products abroad; Firm 'C' (10 employees) produces silver sculptures and sells 10% of them abroad; Firm 'D' (6 employees) produces ceramics, with 70% export; and finally Firm 'E' (9 employees) produces machine-woven tapestries and blankets and has no significant exports. They are all of a similar size and their products are complementary insofar as they are consistent in style, but different in terms of type, use and value.

Despite their small size, membership of the consortium allows the firms to promote their sales abroad (especially in the USA and Europe) using selected distribution channels to reach customers interested in Peruvian-style goods.

The competitive strategy of Muyu is essentially a focus strategy as all of its products are markedly characterized by their ethnic profile, though developed in accordance with modern concepts and forms. The customer preferences targeted by Muyu, therefore, must be consistent with Peruvian culture and tradition and its products are directed towards a narrow international customer segment.

Consistently with its focus strategy, the consortium uses selected channels specializing in handicrafts, mainly aimed at the USA and European markets (Germany, Holland, Belgium and Spain). Although to a lesser extent, it also promotes its products in Chile and Bolivia. In foreign countries, the products are usually sold in museums, art galleries, boutiques and fair trade association outlets.

The strategic positioning of Muyu is clearly summarized in its formal mission statement: *'to satisfy the functional, ornamental and fashion needs of demanding markets through handmade products, styled according to ancestral Peruvian tradition, but proposed in modern forms'*. The 'typical Peruvian style' and 'locally handmade artisan manufacturing' are key elements of the consortium's strategy and drive all of its promotional activities. In the case of Muyu such elements become location-specific strategic resources and reinforce the competitive advantage of the member firms and the consortium in their markets.

With regard to the core promotional activity of the consortium, the formal strategic market objectives of Muyu are: to *increase the competitiveness of its member firms* by organizing their offer and ensuring effective trade promotion; to *achieve better positioning and larger market shares* in both the domestic and international markets; to establish the consortium's *brand 'Muyu Peru' as a symbol of quality*.

However, in addition to its commercial objectives, the consortium also has internal objectives that are more centred on the development of the individual firms and the efficiency of the network: (a) to plan and implement product innovation; (b) to increase productivity and standardize the production of member firms; (c) to develop competences and managerial tools for improving the profitability of member firms by means of greater efficiency and increased sales.

The consortium's main marketing activities are participation in specialized trade fairs and showroom product range presentations.

The consortium's financial resources derive directly from the members, who contribute to the budget in two ways, firstly, via a fixed, equal annual amount to cover operating costs and secondly, by specific contributions to the cost of individual activities or projects (such as participating in trade fairs) which are divided equally among the firms actually taking part. Given the small size and limited resources of the member firms, and in keeping with its nature as a promotional export consortium, Muyu does not have its own premises or offices.

The consortium also fosters inter-organizational learning and knowledge-sharing. The learning outcomes are particularly relevant in two areas – the development of the collections and the compilation of the product catalogue, and the creation of a shared database of suppliers and customers. Design, fashion and product development courses are complemented by workshops focusing on image marketing.

The enhancement of the firms' marketing and promotional competences is one of the main outcomes of participation in the consortium. This has led to a significant increase in export sales. Exports to the USA and EU now account for 40% of total sales, and foreign sales by the five micro enterprises have more than doubled since the consortium was founded. In addition, as a result of their participation in the consortium, member firms also improved their market reputation and benefited from easier access to technical assistance and training programmes promoted by public and private institutions.

4.7　Peruvian Bio Consortia (Peru)

The members of Peruvian Bio Consortia were selected in mid-2006 by the Peruvian Institute of Natural Products (IPPN). Originally, the group consisted of five firms offering products to industrial and consumer markets (especially products with functional characteristics), though two firms withdrew shortly afterwards.

The remaining three member firms, all family businesses, are: Firm 'A', established in 1980, with 21 employees and producing liquid and dry plant extracts for cosmetic use, functional food, oils and personal hygiene care products (with exports of 60% of total sales); Firm 'B', established in 1985, with 37 employees and specializing in natural nutritional and cosmetic products (exporting 10%); and Firm 'C', established in 2001, with 27 employees and producing nutritional products (dry herbs, fruits and vegetables), 90% of which are sold on foreign markets. They are currently planning to recruit new firms on the basis of specific selection criteria, including unanimous agreement of the founder members.

The 'vision' of Peruvian Bio Consortia may be summarized as follows: *'To be a consolidated consortium with a solid resource base, leading innovation within the sector, protecting the environment, and generating economic development'*.

The main functions of the consortium are to promote the firms and their products, prepare advertising and promotional materials, organize participation in international fairs and exhibitions and in other pro-export activities (such as trade missions), organize training courses and establish partnerships with other organizations.

As agricultural product processing firms, the members compete in the same markets and distribution channels. However, in order to avoid internal competition within the consortium, the group has assessed the strengths of each firm and identified those member firms' products to be promoted by the consortium. In defining the product range of the consortium, a significant role was played by the three firms with international experience. The USA, Europe and, residually, Japan were identified as target markets.

The consortium structure is extremely simple. The meetings of the board are held at the premises of Firm 'A', whose representative is also president of the consortium. All of the member firms have their own leaders and their roles are well integrated within the consortium. There is significant information exchange and knowledge sharing and decisions are made on the basis of a simple majority. Member firms are also familiar with each other's production facilities and assist each other with production activities when necessary.

Peruvian Bio Consortia has therefore no equity on its balance sheet. Member firms have decided to provide financial contributions to the consortium only when a specific activity has been (or needs to be) carried out. The costs of such activities are divided among the member firms.

The consortium's main impact has been on the improved image and reputation of the member firms. Peruvian Bio Consortia has managed to establish itself as the leading consortium in Peru in the natural products sector. As a result, representatives of the member firms are often invited to give talks at conferences, above all to describe their experience in the bio-products market.

Despite the difficulties in determining whether the good performance of the member firms in 2007 can be directly ascribed to their participation in the consortium, Peruvian Bio Consortia has undoubtedly improved their negotiating capacity and market power on the international market. In terms of members' perceptions of the consortium's achievement of its strategic goals, all three firms agree that they are positively perceived by supporting institutions and, in particular, that their export promotion activities have substantially increased. On average, firms' sales increased by 20% due to greater export activity. Furthermore, the consortium has increased the members' pro-export activities, particularly in terms of their participation in international export fairs in South America (Brazil), Europe (Switzerland) and the USA.

Peruvian Bio Consortia has become the leading consortium for natural products in Peru and is considered to be an example of cooperation for other firms in the sector. In March 2008, the consortium was ranked second in the 'Export Production Chain' category of a national corporate social responsibility competition. Finally, in terms of resources and competences of the member firms, they have experienced major improvements in marketing and technical competences, as well as in their image among customers and suppliers.

4.8 ACMC (Peru)

ACMC Industrial Group is a sales export consortium of metal and engineering firms founded in mid-2007 by the Peruvian Ministry of Production (PRODUCE).

It comprises four small firms: Firm 'A' (53 employees) produces metal furniture for private and business use; Firm 'B' (18 employees) designs and manufactures machinery for the metal furniture sector; Firm 'C' (15 employees) produces decorative items, metal furniture and metal carpentry tools; Firm 'D' (35 employees) manufactures metal furniture for exhibitions (display stands and similar products). All the firms are located within the Villa del Salvador industrial estate, which is the only one in the city of Lima. Member firms have similar production facilities and are therefore able to manufacture similar products in order to increase their overall export potential. They also have significant export experience.

The ACMC firms combined both their production facilities and more than 15 years of experience in the sector with the aim of offering a greater variety of customized quality products at competitive prices. They are vertically integrated, from the design phase to the production of moulds and finished products, thus ensuring complete quality control. This integration also allows them to increase production easily and reduce lead times.

4.8 ACMC (Peru)

They hold a consolidated product position within the local market and their products are sold nationally to well-known public and private firms, while exports on total sales range between 5% and 10%. This position was established not only due to the quality of the products, but also owing to a proven reliability in business transactions.

The consortium's strategic vision states that it aims '*to be solid and professionally managed, to contribute to the country's social and economic development, and to attain a strong position in national and international market, by developing new products and markets, using appropriate technological resources in order to offer quality products under both its own brand and international certification*'.

The main functions of the ACMC consortium may be summarized as follows: the joint promotion of the firms and joint sale of their products; the creation of promotional materials and marketing campaigns (such as participation in international trade fairs, trade missions, and meetings with potential commercial partners); training activities; the establishment of partnerships with other cooperative institutions; participation in local public calls for tender.

Furthermore, the consortium exploits its participation in trade fairs in order to promote its members' products, especially among wholesalers, retailers and importers. The main target markets are Latin American (especially the Andean region), where the firms have already built up substantial experience.

At a very early stage in the life of ACMC, it was decided to establish an organizational structure in which each entrepreneur would be responsible for a specific function: Firm 'A' for Institutional and Public Relations; Firm 'B' for Projects; Firm 'C' for Administration; Firm 'D' for Marketing and Sales. The owner behind company 'A' is also president of the consortium. After the increase in local sales and the decision to export, the entrepreneurs decided to hire a managing director for the consortium. The shares in the consortium are divided proportionally among the members. Group membership is closed, but the consortium establishes partnerships with local companies for specific projects. The consortium's operating costs are paid proportionally by the member firms and there is a strong orientation to cost reduction. In line with this, meetings of the consortium are held in the offices of one of the member firms in order to reduce costs.

As a result of the consortium's activities, the firms have improved and intensified their promotional strategies in foreign markets, especially participation in international trade fairs, starting with those held in South America. Export promotion activities started in 2007 and are progressing quite rapidly, despite the absence of public financial support, with the consortium about to enter neighbouring markets such as Bolivia and Ecuador. Prior to 2007, only one firm was running pro-export campaigns. The firms are also collaborating with the Ministry of Production in a programme aimed at creating a network of suppliers.

Although the full impact of these efforts cannot yet be appreciated, the prospects are encouraging: the consortium is more established in the local market, especially in terms of calls for tender, and the joint actions of the four members have led to significant improvements in the overall quality of products, as well as in their confidence in both themselves and each other. In particular, the image of the consortium is seen as an important resource, which also benefits the individual firms.

Throughout all of its activities, the consortium has pursued two main goals: to strengthen the group's identity and image, and increase foreign market penetration. However, given also its short time in existence (just under 2 years), the results so far achieved by the member firms have mainly concerned local markets. Domestic sales by individual firms in 2008 increased by 100% compared to 2007.

The perception of the member firms concerning the achievement of the consortium strategic goals is that they have managed both to increase production to fulfil emerging market demand and to improve their managerial capabilities, especially with regard to foreign sales development. However, they still need to acquire greater negotiating power on international markets, and improve the organizational structure of the consortium in order to make for more streamlined management.

4.9 Ande Natura (Peru)

Ande Natura is a promotional consortium, established in June 2007 and composed of five very small family firms. They offer a variety of products within the aromatic herb and organic food sector: Firm 'A' (12 employees) produces aromatic herbs, filtered infusions and has an export intensity of 20%; Firm 'B' (9 employees) produces green and black tea and its exports account for 10% of sales; Firm 'C' (2 employees) produces Sacha Inchi oil, jams and cereals and has a 6% export intensity; Firm 'D' (4 employees) produces local potatoes as snacks and exports 10% of its production; finally Firm 'E' (the largest, with 40 employees) produces organic coffee, annatto and palillo colorants, and has an export intensity of 98%.

Ande Natura was originally founded by Firm 'A' and two NGOs, who were more interested in developing educational programmes than entrepreneurial activities. These differences in the strategic vision of the network led to the departure of the NGOs.

All of the member firms have an agro-industrial profile and operate in the organic food sector. The production base is therefore the land, and processing takes place within the region. Their products are not in direct competition as they originate from different plants, vegetables and herbs, and range from filtered infusions to oils, crisps and jams, among others. In this way, they complement the consortium's portfolio and improve the overall offer, making it attractive to customers owing to its quality. The products can benefit from higher prices ('premium price') as they are organic, are of a higher quality, and target customers are in the Fair Trade niche market.

The consortium does not replace the entrepreneurial initiative of its members. Rather, Ande Natura acts as an umbrella brand and is used for promotional activities. Each firm's brand is promoted and each firm handles its own purchase and sales contracts. The USA and Europe are the prospective foreign markets for all of the member firms. The consortium endeavours to exploit all previously-established business connections.

The mission of the consortium is summarized thus, '*an association linked to growing markets, developing quality food products, supporting the organic food production chain and promoting the sustainable use of resources through the adoption of agro-ecological practices*'.

While the consortium's overall goal is '*to establish a self-sustainable export consortium of organic food producers in the south-east macro-region of the country*', it also has some more specific objectives: (a) to develop an environmentally sustainable offer of products derived from aromatic, oleaginous and tuberose plants, and Andean corns; (b) to improve the revenues of member firms through export and transfer the benefits to the production base by applying the principles of fair trade; (c) to develop the technological and organizational characteristics needed to satisfy the requirements of the organic products sector in the global market; (d) to promote sustainable productive bases, grow varieties of species for which there is a market demand and reduce the costs of the certification process.

Ande Natura has identified and defined these strategic objectives via a formal strategic planning process. The consortium also has some managerial objectives: to develop the necessary managerial capabilities and tools for developing new markets; to strengthen the financial aspects of member firms and to improve profits by increasing sales and reducing operational costs.

The consortium is managed by a *junta coordinadora* (management board) consisting of one representative from each firm: a coordinator, three associate managers and a treasurer. The initial coordinator of the group was chosen for his marketing experience and business ties with one of the NGOs that sponsored the creation of the consortium. The good personal relationships which exist among the entrepreneurs also favour the smooth management of the consortium. Internal regulations have also played a crucial role in problem-solving, helping the members to avoid the conflicts that can arise within a consortium.

The meetings of the consortium take place on a weekly basis at the offices of one of the firms. The agenda is decided upon during the previous week's meeting and decisions are always taken unanimously. In accordance with the consortium's regulations, fines are levied for failing to attend these meetings. Mutual trust and confidence among members have increased over time as a result of the development of joint activities. One important factor in improving trust has been the creation of a diversified and complementary portfolio of products. This choice has proved to be successful as foreign buyers usually prefer to deal with an organization which offers a wide variety of different and innovative products, rather than with a number of smaller firms.

All of the firms agree that the Ande Natura brand has been successfully promoted and that the consortium's market power has been strengthened on international markets. Since the consortium was constituted, the member firms estimate an 85% increase in sales. Contacts with prospective customers have also grown as a result of participation in the most important international fairs for the food industry (e.g. Brazil, USA, Switzerland and Spain). Other achievements of the consortium include: an improvement in outsourced services as a result of a more efficient exchange of information among those firms which cultivate aromatic plants, a reduction in marketing costs and stronger relationships with public and private institutions. In this respect, it is worthy noting that the consortium's export initiatives are supported financially by public export promotion institutions such as PROMPERU and DIRCETUR, as well as the NGO, IMAGEN. Finally, there has been an increase in the number of personnel employed by the firms. This has reached an annual growth rate of 5% and is likely to increase further still as a result of greater export activity.

4.10 Phyto Uruguay (Uruguay)

The consortium Phyto Uruguay, established in 2005, has nine members, mostly micro-enterprises, operating in the herbal and nutraceutical products sector: Firm 'A' (5 employees) produces food integrators; Firm 'B' (27 employees) produces organic herbs; Firm 'C' (67 employees) produces cosmetics; Firm 'D' (10 employees) produces herbal and natural pharmaceutics; Firm 'E' (10 employees) produces homeopathic products, cosmetics, veterinary homeopathic products and essential oils; Firm 'F' (12 employees) produces cosmetics; Firm 'G' (7 employees) produces aloe; Firm 'H' (20 employees) produces dietary products, functional food, medicaments; Firm 'I' (5 employees) produces vegetable extracts. The firms' main distribution channels are retailers and wholesalers, pharmacies and perfumeries. In 2009 three further firms were about to join the consortium.

Promoted by UNIDO, this consortium was also supported by FUNDASOL, a non-profit association promoting Uruguayan businesses, in cooperation with other institutions such as the Interamerican Development Bank (IDB), the Ecumenical Economic Development Cooperative Society (OIKOCREDIT), the Interamerica Foundation (IAF), the German Cooperation (GTZ) and UNESCO.

It is worth noting that – with the exception of one firm (with a 9.4% export intensity) – none of the member firms had any previous export experience. They did not participate in international trade fairs, had no knowledge of international payment tools and showed little compliance with international standards. Moreover, none of the firms employed an export manager, and only a minority had dedicated sales staff.

The firms' internationalization strategies started with Phyto Uruguay. The consortium supports member firms in promoting their products abroad through participation in overseas trade fairs. Target markets and related promotional activities are chosen by the members on the basis of their previous experience.

The group is managed by a president chosen among the member entrepreneurs and is supported by a secretary and external business consultants. Weekly meetings are organized and held at Fundasol's offices. The consortium's structure is mainly financed by member firms through a 3% commission on sales made by the consortium and members' contributions for specific services.

In addition to promoting the products of member firms under its own brand, the consortium invests in quality improvement by implementing quality standards throughout the value chain and creating a jointly-operated research laboratory. Furthermore, the products of the consortium are to be certified as 'Bio-Phyto' by the Italian Institute for Ethical and Environmental Certification (ICEA).

The link between higher exports and upgrading the organizational and managerial structure of the firms would appear to be extremely strong indeed. As a consequence of being part of the consortium, all member firms have revamped their packaging and increased their bargaining power with suppliers. They are now taking advantage of their greater bargaining power as a group to develop the national market and are negotiating with large-scale Uruguayan retail buyers. In addition, the majority have also revised their products and promotional material, and invested in new equipment and technologies. Almost all the firms have obtained or are in the process of obtaining international certification, such as ISO 9001 and GMP (Good Manufacturing Practices). The global turnover of most members has increased in recent years and half have taken on more staff.

Finally, the effective combination of upgrading the firms' manufacturing processes and promotional activities implemented by the consortium is already producing positive effects: Phyto Uruguay has recently signed a commercial agreement with an Italian customer.

References

Chetty, S., & Holm, D. B. (2000). Internationalisation of small to medium-sized manufacturing firms: A network approach. *International Business Review, 9*(1), 77–93.
Eisenhardt, K. (1989). Building theories from case study research. *Academy of Management Review, 14*(4), 532–550.
Pfeffer, J. (2009). Renaissance and renewal in management studies: Relevance regained. *European Management Review, 6*(3), 141–148.
Yin, R. (1989). *Case study research, design and methods*. Beverley Hills: Sage.

The Management of Export Consortia: A Pragmatic Approach

5.1 A Framework for the Analysis of Export Consortium Management

As discussed in Chap. 3, consortia have specific characteristics which differentiate them from other types of network. A specific approach is necessary in order to understand the strategic behaviour and management of consortia. Building on the empirical evidence presented in Chap. 4, we develop a framework for analyzing the management of export consortia. We also describe certain strategic management tools that can assist consortia executives in formulating and implementing effective strategies as well as monitoring performance.

Managing an export consortium is by no means an easy task and raises a number of issues related to the multiple ties among the member firms, generally SMEs. Furthermore, as consortium initiatives may be beneficial to member firms to varying degrees, both the formulation and implementation of consortium strategy are crucial. In particular, the strategy must not clash with the needs and objectives of individual members.

The goal of an export consortium is to support member firms in exploiting business opportunities in international markets and help them overcome the constraints they may experience due to their limited size.

On the one hand, an export consortium is characterized by a number of small firms with different backgrounds, strategies and business models, as well as different sets of resources and competences. These differences also involve the international experience of the firms. Although it is assumed that the members of an export consortium are at the initial stages of internationalization, their export experience may vary considerably.

On the other hand, the competitive challenge for these firms is to make the most of the trading opportunities on foreign markets in order to increase their chances of survival and growth. Through participation in an export consortium, SMEs pool their resources and develop a formal strategic interfirm network in order to tackle the internationalization process. From the very beginning, it is necessary that the rationale for the consortium is clear to all of the member firms. The gaps in resources and competences which need to be filled must be identified, and members must be aware that these gaps cannot be filled via stand-alone strategies.

The decision to set up a consortium implies major choices in terms of strategy and organization, which are summarized in Fig. 5.1. The strategic goals and

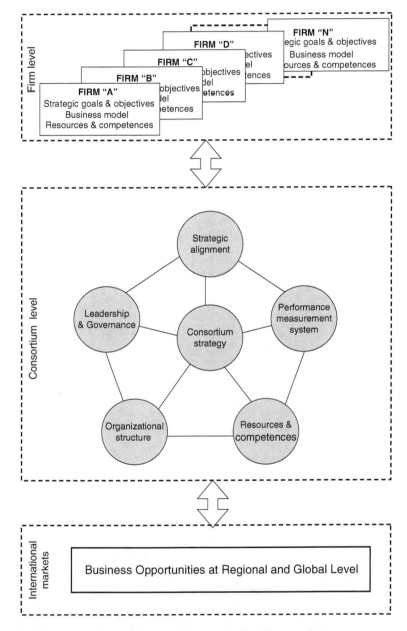

Fig. 5.1 A framework for analyzing the management of export consortia

5.1 A Framework for the Analysis of Export Consortium Management

objectives, business models, resources and competences of member firms affect both what they expect to receive from the consortium as well as their capacity to contribute to it. These elements need to be carefully analyzed before the alliance is formalized in order to assess the strategic alignment among members. In fact, management problems may arise from a lack of strategic convergence due to the differing objectives of the member firms. This happens, for example, when some partners wish to become stable players in a foreign market and are willing to commit resources to the alliance, while others display a short-term perspective (such as seeing consortium membership merely as an opportunity to sell temporary production surpluses) and may, therefore, be unwilling to commit financial and human resources to the development of the alliance over time.

The central area of Fig. 5.1 shows the main areas which the strategic management of a consortium must cover:
- Strategic alignment of member firms
- Consortium strategy and actions
- Organizational structure
- Leadership and governance systems
- Resources and competences
- Performance measurement system

The strategy of an export consortium should address the following questions:
- What are the consortium's goals and objectives? Which activities will enable the consortium to reach those goals and objectives?
- What is the consortium's value proposition? (The answer to this question will depend on whether it is a promotional or sales consortium – see Sect. 5.3).
- What gaps need to be filled in order to successfully implement the formulated strategy? (Gaps or 'strategic needs' may be related to financial and technological issues, knowledge and capabilities and/or human resources. These needs will be satisfied in different ways depending on the characteristics of the firms. For example, the presence of a member firm with international experience may lead to the decision to appoint a representative of that firm as general manager of the consortium, whereas this position would probably be filled by an external candidate should none of the partner firms have experience of foreign markets).

In order to answer these questions, the consortium must analyze the environment and identify both the barriers to export that need to be overcome and, more generally, the principal environmental trends and how they are likely to affect the consortium strategy over time.

All of the factors shown in the centre of the model represented in Fig. 5.1 need to be consistent with the characteristics of the member firms. The consortium performance will be considered satisfactory if the strategy and operations are in line with the international business opportunities which the member firms wish to pursue. Measuring performance is crucial, as the consortium strategy may be reinforced or modified on the basis of results, and the way individual member firms perceive the benefits and costs associated with the alliance may affect their own goals and behaviour and, consequently, influence their alignment.

As Fig. 5.1 shows, not only 'top-down' relationships but also a set of bidirectional relationships exist among the factors presented in the framework. In this chapter we analyze each of the elements of the framework in detail and focus on the following activities which are related to the setting-up and management of export consortia:

- Managing the strategic alignment of member firms
- Formulating consortium strategy
- Designing the organizational structure
- Leveraging on strategic resources and competences
- Enforcing corporate governance and leadership
- Measuring consortium performance

In order to bridge theory and practice, we will refer extensively (either in the text or in separate boxes) to examples drawn from the export consortia covered in our empirical analysis and presented in detail in Chap. 4.

5.2 Managing the Strategic Alignment of Member Firms

The strategic alignment of member firms is one of the key factors affecting the success of a consortium. Alignment must not only be assessed when the partners are selected, but also monitored throughout the life of the consortium. At the start-up stage, a preliminary assessment of the potential members should be carried out in order to evaluate whether, and to what extent, their strategic convergence is possible.

In the case of SMEs, the task of assessing the *ex ante* strategic alignment is normally carried out by external 'network facilitators' (McEvily and Zaheer 2004), such as associations of firms, public agencies, and other public or private agents. Network facilitators foster collaboration within a network as they help partners to build trust-based relationships (see Sect. 2.7). In the export consortia covered by our analysis, UNIDO played the role of network facilitator. In some cases, UNIDO worked in collaboration with local public institutions. This was the case of *GET IT* (Box 5.1), where an important process of trust-building preceded the launching of the consortium. Similarly, the support of the UNIDO Export Consortia Programme was also crucial in the case of *Phyto Uruguay*. The initial efforts of *Phyto Uruguay* were focused on the enhancement of trust-based relationships among member firms and the definition of joint objectives, leveraging on the support of UNIDO and FUNDASOL (a non-profit association for the promotion of Uruguayan firms). In addition, *Phyto Uruguay* also benefited from the UNIDO Trade Capacity Building programme aimed at upgrading the technical and organizational structure of member firms. This programme played an important role in enabling firms to develop an exportable offer complying with international standards.

Assessing strategic alignment is not necessarily the result of a rational, formal analysis. The values and culture of entrepreneurs, as well as personal relationships, are also of importance. A number of firm-specific factors do, however, need to be taken into account in the selection process of member firms. These include:

(a) Strategic medium- and long-term goals and short-term objectives
(b) Time-horizon of the internationalization process of member firms
(c) Competitive strategy and positioning
(d) Resources and competences
(e) Commitment to cooperation
(f) Organizational culture

(a) Strategic medium- and long-term goals and short-term objectives. Convergence of the strategic goals and objectives of the member firms is crucial for the success of the alliance. 'Hidden agendas' represent the greatest risk, and some networks fail because the true goals and objectives of the partners differ from those declared. This is the case when one firm endeavours to obtain advantages to the detriment of the others, or when important information is not shared. Trying to understand the real objectives of partner firms is therefore necessary, and it is often the 'network facilitator' who is tasked with this responsibility.

(b) The time-horizon of the internationalization process of member firms. Problems of alignment can arise from differences in the firms' internationalization time-horizons. Difficulties in making decisions about timing and the amount of investments, as well as the new markets to enter, may arise when some firms wish to go international quickly, while others favour a more gradual approach. The importance of internationalization as a long-term strategy may also be perceived differently by individual partners. *Mosaic* is an interesting case in point. The member firms are all of a similar size and are positioned within the same industry; they have substantial export experience and are capable of operating in international markets. In addition, their strategic orientation is fairly similar; all the firms are subcontractors of international corporations and aim to increase their capacity to operate autonomously in international markets by developing end products suitable for international customers. These conditions have increased the strategic alignment of the partners. However, the group of firms that launched the consortium in 2004 was not so homogeneous. It included a number of small firms that soon realized that they were unable to follow the ambitious action plan supported by the larger firms and hence left the consortium. They were then replaced by larger and more experienced members. As a result of this change, a greater homogeneity among firms was achieved in terms of size, sector and foreign market competences. Their products also displayed high complementarity in terms of customer needs. The profiles and interests of the member firms therefore became increasingly aligned, creating a highly favourable environment for developing shared consortium strategies.

(c) Competitive strategy and positioning. The compatibility of parties in an alliance is highly dependent on their strategies. We can use the example of a group of firms from the same industry who decide to combine their efforts in order to enter foreign markets. Alignment will be greater if those firms use the same distribution channels, have similar quality standards, and if their products are complementary – offering a full range to international customers. Conversely, alignment will be difficult to achieve if partners differ substantially in areas such as product quality, competitive positioning and domestic reputation.

(d) Resources and competences. A key question to be addressed is whether, and to what extent, the resources and competences which partners are able to commit to the network are enough to ensure an integrated portfolio, consistent with the challenges of international competition. The main reason why SMEs cooperate through a consortium is to pool their resources and efforts in order to achieve a goal which could not be achieved efficiently by any of the firms individually. The implementation of any strategy (including a consortium strategy) relies on a set of resources and capabilities. An assessment of the resources and capabilities that partners are able to contribute to the network is therefore necessary both to prevent any imbalance in terms of partner commitment and to identify those resources which need to be sourced from outside the network itself.

(e) Commitment to cooperation. Commitment to cooperation is necessary as all the firms are expected to invest in the start-up and growth of the consortium. As pointed out by Wilkinson and Mattson (1994: 22), '[...] *individual network participants must be committed to their development. No amount of government incentives, encouragement and exhortations will substitute for a clearly perceived logic of relationship formation by the parties involved and beneficial outcomes.*' If commitment to cooperation is low, there is a risk that alignment will be highly unstable.

(f) Culture. Cultural differences are usually responsible for a lack of strategic alignment, and have been identified as one of the major causes of alliance failure (Troy 1994). Organizational culture is affected by various factors, such as firm size, nationality, and business models. We can therefore expect that export consortia whose partners are similar in these areas will have fewer problems in terms of strategic alignment than those with more heterogeneous partners. In the case of SMEs, organizational culture is also particularly influenced by the entrepreneur's education, professional background and values. The case of *Get 'IT* demonstrates that previous reciprocal knowledge encourages partners to share the same values. The foundation of this consortium was the result of a previous 1-year period of informal cooperation among six firms interested in carrying out internationalization activities financed by the Tunisian National Fund for the Access to Export Markets (FAMEX). The consortium was then formally established with the support of UNIDO in partnership with the Tunisian Ministry of Industry, Energy and SMEs (see Box 5.1).

Box 5.1: The Strategic Alignment of *Get'IT* Member Firms

Get'IT was officially launched in 2005 and was the first IT consortium set up in Tunisia. It now consists of 11 firms operating in the field of Information and Communication Technologies (ICT), which has recently been one of the fastest-growing industries in the Tunisian economy. The consortium was founded as a result of a previous one-year experience of cooperation that began informally as a 'common journey' of six firms interested in going international. A high level of mutual trust among the firms motivated them to

> formalize their alliance. The consortium benefited from the support of UNIDO and the Tunisian Ministry of Industry, Energy and SMEs.
> Although they are all ICT service providers, the partner firms are of significantly different sizes, and there is little competition between them as their markets do not overlap. Furthermore, their products are complementary, offering a broad range of services.
> The success of the consortium strategy is demonstrated mostly by its aggregative ability, which led to an increase in member numbers from six to eleven in just 3 years. The 'networking rationale' works particularly well in this case for a number of reasons:
> (a) All of the firms belong to one industry – ICT – which, by its very nature, emphasizes communication and integration.
> (b) Given the specialization of the member firms in different fields and market segments, there is very little competition between their products.
> (c) Finally, 'networking' is a familiar concept to the firms: Most of the solutions the firms implement for their customers are the result of collaboration; network-based organizational models are very common among ICT firms; networking is a basic concept for all digital and web-based technologies. 'Networking' can therefore be considered a key feature of the firms' business models.

Issues related to the strategic alignment of member firms may also arise at any stage of the life of the consortium. This strategic alignment should therefore be continuously monitored. After a consortium begins implementing projects, a variety of changes may take place within member firms affecting their growth patterns and relationships with the other firms. This requires changes in the make-up of the consortium itself. Alignment must also be taken into account whenever there is an opportunity to involve a new partner in the alliance.

The alignment of the competitive strategies of independent businesses evolves into the development of a shared vision of future international activities which clearly expresses the reasons underlying the alliance and the advantages which each member can obtain from the network. For example, *Peruvian Bio* has developed a clear vision that may be summarized as follows: '*To be a consolidated consortium with a solid resource base, leading innovation within the sector, protecting the environment, and generating economic development*'. Building a clear vision is crucial as '[...] *companies that enjoy enduring success have core values and a core purpose that remain fixed while their business strategies and practices endlessly adapt to a changing world.*' (Collins and Porras 1996: 65). A well-conceived vision consists of two elements, a core ideology and an envisioned future. The core ideology defines '*what we stand for and why we exist*', while the envisioned future is '*what we aspire to become, to create*' (Collins and Porras 1996). The ability to develop a consortium vision depends to a great extent on the presence of a leader.

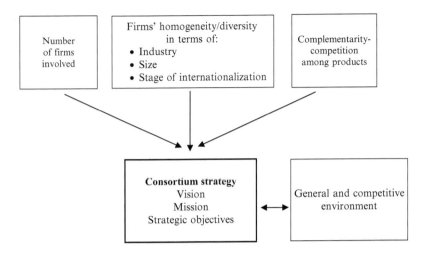

Fig. 5.2 Characteristics of member firms and their impact on consortium strategy

This may either be one of the partner entrepreneurs or an external specialist specifically hired to manage the consortium.

The degree of ease or difficulty with which a shared vision can be developed, and a strategic alignment reached and sustained over time, is affected by the following factors (Fig. 5.2):

(a) Number of partners involved in the alliance.
(b) Homogeneity of the member firms in terms of:
  • Industry
  • Size
  • Stage of internationalization
(c) Degree of complementarity/competition among the products of member firms.

(a) The number of firms involved in an alliance is one of the main determinants of its complexity. Consortia with a very high number of partners cannot usually involve all of them in formulating strategy, and are managed in a similar way to large organizations via a more complex organizational structure. The higher the number of partners, the higher the number of potentially different visions and missions. In the consortia launched with the support of UNIDO, the number of member firms is relatively low. Consortium size is not a key issue today, but may become relevant in the future.

(b) The degree of homogeneity/diversity within the network is important as it affects identification of common missions and goals. Homogeneity must first be evaluated at industry level. In the case of diverse industries, it is necessary to identify strategic business areas within the consortium as if it were a multi-business firm, and a specific strategy needs to be formulated and implemented for each. Furthermore, when the partners do not offer complementary products, a high degree of diversification in terms of products and customers may become an issue given

5.2 Managing the Strategic Alignment of Member Firms

that a number of costs cannot be shared. In each of the export consortia covered by our empirical analysis, member firms either belong to the same industry or are vertically integrated. This factor reduces the level of complexity. However, the degree of heterogeneity may increase over time as a result of changes in the composition of the consortium.

Differences in size can be an obstacle to formulating strategy as specific visions and goals may be size-related. The size of firms also affects availability of financial and human resources. Small firms are likely to make lower investments, and differing degrees of willingness to invest in the consortium can greatly affect the growth of the alliance. Small firms generally also lack sophisticated competences, particularly in the area of internationalization. Alliances which include both smaller and larger firms can be positive due to their complementary nature. However, there is a greater risk of network instability.

The *stage of internationalization of member firms* is another factor that must be taken into account. Shared goals in terms of international development are easy to define if member firms are in more or less the same phase, but this may be more difficult when they are at different stages of their internationalization process. Less internationalized firms can learn much from more internationalized partners. However, the latter also need to see the alliance as beneficial. For example, benefits for more internationalized firms arise when those which are less internationalized supply complementary products and services, have developed innovations which make the consortium's value proposition more appealing, or can supply the network with resources that are scarce or difficult to develop.

(c) Finally, the degree of complementarity/competition among the products of member firms must be assessed. A high level of complementarity may be considered positive for aligning the vision, mission and goal of a network. *Get'IT* is a good example of complementary services, where 11 partners from the same industry supply different offers (see Box 5.1). Defining a consortium strategy when members' products are in direct competition with each other in the domestic market can be more difficult. *Travel Partner* is an example of a consortium of domestic competitors who cooperate at an international level. In this case a focus strategy is likely to be more successful than one with a broader scope (see Sect. 5.3 for an analysis of consortium strategies).

Consortium strategy is influenced by the external environment and closely related to the consortium's vision, mission and strategic objectives. A consortium's mission defines its identity and its main purpose. As Hax and Majluf (1991: 47) point out, *'the mission of the business defines the competitive domain in terms of business scope (products, markets, and geographical locations), as well as unique competences that determine the key capabilities of the business'*. Similarly, mission may be defined as the *'declaration of what a firm is and what it stands for – its fundamental values and purpose'* (Carpenter and Sanders 2008: 46). In the case of *Muyu*, for example, their mission has been defined thus: *'To satisfy the functional, ornamental and fashion needs of demanding markets through handmade products, styled according to ancestral Peruvian tradition, but proposed in modern forms'*.

When member firms have a clear idea of both vision and mission, they are able both to build consensus about consortium strategy at the beginning of its life, and maintain it over time. Vision and mission also inform key stakeholders (internal and external) about the path of growth the consortium will follow. The mission and vision of a consortium are therefore fundamental to the formulation of its strategy, and reinforce the strategy itself.

Strategic objectives are medium- to long-term objectives which provide a bridge between vision and strategy (Carpenter and Sanders 2008) and need to be quantifiable in order that the extent to which the consortium strategy is satisfying the expectations which are at the root of its foundation may be assessed. Typical long-term objectives may be:

(a) For a promotional consortium: the number of contacts with international customers, the number of countries visited, the number of other business networks joined, the number of contacts with large-scale distributors abroad.
(b) For a sales consortium: the revenues generated abroad (in general and within specific foreign markets in particular), profits, the number of foreign customers, overseas reputation and image.

Formulating an effective strategy requires a profound understanding of the external environment, which is simultaneously a source of threats and business opportunities. The environment can be broadly defined as encompassing a variety of economic and socio-political factors or, more narrowly, as a firm's market arena. Knowledge of both industry- and firm-specific factors is therefore critical in order to identify viable strategies and understand the competitive positions member firms can achieve.

5.3 Formulating Consortium Strategy

As with other cooperative ventures, consortia need a strategy which is both independent from, but consistent with, those of the member firms. The competitive strategy of a consortium (especially a sales consortium) is very similar to that of any individual firm wishing to enter international markets. A 'business idea' (Normann 1977) has therefore to be developed by responding to the following questions:

- What is the consortium value proposition in its target international markets?
- Who are the target customers of the products and services offered by the consortium?
- What activities will the consortium carry out? And what resources and competences will the consortium exploit?

Given that a consortium is the result of an alliance between already existing firms, the range of products it can offer in the international arena is not difficult to define. Firstly, it is necessary to list all of the partners' products and decide which are most suitable for the target foreign market(s).

Before deciding which products to sell abroad, any possible overlap needs to be identified. An overlap is more likely if the consortium's members are in

5.3 Formulating Consortium Strategy

competition with each other. For example, as agricultural product processing firms, the members of *Peruvian Bio* compete in the same markets and distribution channels for sales and supplies. In order to avoid possible conflicts, the group has assessed each firm's competitive advantage and then selected a limited range of products to be promoted by the consortium.

In the case of a multi-sector consortium, overlaps are less likely. However, it is still necessary to select the products in order to develop a complete, internally consistent and attractive offer to foreign customers. Product selection must derive from a clear understanding of the requirements of the customers the consortium is endeavouring to attract. Products form part of the consortium value proposition, which also includes services and other commercial conditions (such as prices and payment terms). As far as consistency is concerned, the standard of quality of the products offered by different partners, for example, must be very similar.

In the case of promotional consortia, member firms represent the 'target' of the consortium strategy. In other words, member firms can be seen as 'internal customers' to whom the services offered by the consortium are addressed. The 'product range' of a promotional consortium is therefore an array of services mainly aimed at the member firms themselves. This is the case of most consortia included in our empirical analysis as they began their activities as promotional consortia. In the case of *Muyu*, consortium services are also offered to stakeholders outside the network. This consortium has carried out a number of activities for its partners, such as educational programmes aimed at improving the knowledge base and competences of member firms. In addition, *Muyu* plays a role in enhancing the development of the technical competences of local firms, and has also started up a non-profit association to support the local community.

Figure 5.3 shows that four consortium strategies can be identified based on two variables: degree of *competition* and degree of *complementarity* among the

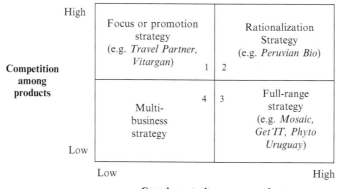

Fig. 5.3 Taxonomy of consortium strategies

products of member firms. *Quadrant 1* represents the case where partner firms are not complementary but in direct competition. This leads to two possibilities. The first is that the consortium merely supports the foreign sales of member firms through generic promotion. *Travel Partner* is an example of a promotion strategy. This consortium comprises seven competing travel agencies which offer basically the same services and are characterized by the same market position. Their small size prevents the individual companies from competing effectively abroad. However, according to most of the entrepreneurs, by operating jointly through the consortium, their image and competitive positioning have improved significantly in relation to both customers and suppliers.

The second option in *Quadrant 1* is a *focus strategy* in which the partners limit their cooperation to a specific area and thus avoid the potential tensions of being in competition (even if only in the domestic market). For example, firms from the same industry could cooperate in a specific geographical market or supply products to specific customers, while competing in other markets or segments. This is the case of *Vitargan*. Member firms are all argan oil producers who have decided to carry out a number of activities jointly in order to achieve economies of scale at specific stages of the supply chain. In this case, information sharing may be limited as partners may be concerned about possible opportunistic behaviour on the part of the other firms.

If the partners are in competition with one another but their products are also complementary, they can adopt a rationalization strategy (*quadrant 2*) by selecting their products and services in such a way as to avoid overlaps and deliver a broad range. *Peruvian Bio* may be considered an example of a rationalization strategy; although members compete in the markets of natural nutritional and cosmetic products, their products also display a certain degree of complementarity. In this strategy, problems arise from the possibility that not all partners will contribute equally in terms of products, and this could lead some of them to underestimate the benefits of the alliance.

A full-range strategy may be more appropriate for consortia in which the products of member firms satisfy the needs of different customers and are characterized by high complementarity (*quadrant 3*). Consortia of this kind need to combine products in order to develop appealing value propositions. Completeness of offer should be their main strength, giving customers the opportunity to deal with just one supplier for a number of products rather than many individual suppliers. As mentioned above, a key factor in successfully implementing this strategy is good alignment of price and product quality among partners. *Mosaic* member firms, for example, are very homogeneous in terms of size, sector and foreign market knowledge, but are highly complementary in relation to customers. A full-range strategy fits the characteristics of this consortium. This is also the case for *Phyto Uruguay*.

Finally, a consortium whose partners' products are neither complementary nor competing (*quadrant 4*) can implement a multi-business strategy. In this case, as partners operate in different industries and are likely to offer products of varying quality, reputation and pricing policy, the key is to identify shared objectives and formulate a strategy that fits the needs of all the members. This situation is very similar to that of a diversified firm in which synergies are weak and difficult to exploit, and different strategies are therefore required for different strategic business areas.

None of the consortia we investigated operate a multi-business strategy. However, if some of the consortia attract firms from different industries in the future, the multi-business strategy could become a strategic option.

Box 5.2: The Strategy of *Phyto Uruguay*

Phyto Uruguay was established in 2005 by Uruguayan SMEs in the herbal and nutraceutical products sector. The consortium presently consists of nine SMEs, and it is probable that three new firms will join the consortium in the near future. The majority are micro-enterprises, though one partner significantly surpasses the others in terms of turnover.

Current marketing strategies are aimed at strengthening the firms' presence in Italy, the most significant foreign market, and fostering expansion in new markets, especially other EU countries and Latin America. Moreover, the consortium has its own brand, which is also a trademark. As well as promotion of the member firms' products under the consortium's own brand *Phyto Uruguay*, the partners are also independently pursuing the promotion of their own products.

After the initial joint promotional activities of the consortium (the principal one being participation in the SANA trade fair in Bologna, Italy), the group decided to organize its operations as a sales consortium, responsible for marketing the products on behalf of its members. The consortium was then incorporated into a public limited company ('Sociedad Anónima') with an equity distributed in equal shares. The main services provided by the consortium include participation in trade fairs, the organization of business missions, the implementation of joint promotional materials, such as a brochure in Spanish, English and Italian, as well as a website. A joint sales department was also set up.

As a sales consortium, *Phyto Uruguay* has branded a specific line of products under the name 'Phyto Uruguay'. The offer includes products belonging to seven different product categories, from raw materials (organic herbs, tea bags, aloe), to essential oils (eucalyptus, mint, Melissa, salvia, calendula, marcela, etc.), herbal extracts (marcela, pitanga, cedròn etc.), natural cosmetics (creams, emulsions, gels etc.) foodstuffs (aloe nectars, powder proteins etc.), nutraceuticals in tablet form (dry extract of grapes, mixed fruits, organic oyster calcium, etc.) and phyto-medicaments in tablet form (focus, garcinia, equinacea etc.). This new line was then promoted abroad through participation at international trade fairs in Italy, Germany, Brazil and Colombia.

Strictly speaking, export consortia are networks for promoting the internationalization of member firms. However, our empirical analysis shows that, while enhancing cooperation for the purposes of internationalization, consortia in developing countries can also create conditions for the effective cooperation of partners at a domestic level. Interview data highlight the fact that, as well as internationalization, another strategic objective has become increasingly important and, in some cases, dominant in these consortia – the upgrading and strengthening of the organizational and managerial structure of member firms. This also leads to the enhancement of the firms' competitiveness in the domestic markets. An increase in 'relational capital' is therefore a major result which can be exploited at home as well as abroad. This strategic objective is particularly important given the lower level of managerial expertise, and limited organizational resources of SMEs in developing countries compared to their counterparts in the developed world.

The empirical evidence shows that consortia are characterized by different combinations of the two strategies that we label 'upgrading' and 'internationalization'. Figure 5.4 shows the 'two-sided' strategy of export consortia in developing countries on the basis of their prevailing strategic objectives.

We can identify three groups of consortia corresponding to three strategic archetypes. As well as 'upgrading' and 'internationalizing', a third group encompasses those consortia whose strategic objective is a balanced combination of the two. In Fig. 5.5 the nine consortia covered by our analysis are positioned on the basis of their prevailing strategic objectives.

The strategic objectives of consortia may change over time as a result of the changing interests and priorities of the member firms, as well as the different stages of the consortium life-cycle. In general, an 'upgrading' objective may be more

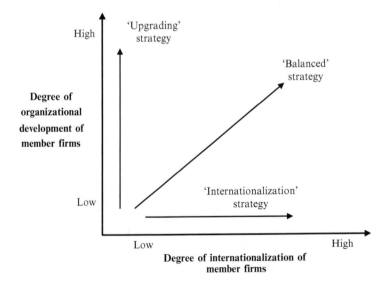

Fig. 5.4 The two-sided strategy of export consortia in developing countries

5.3 Formulating Consortium Strategy

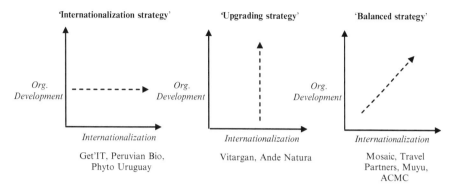

Fig. 5.5 Archetypes of export consortia on the basis of their prevailing strategic objectives

common and important for smaller firms and represent the first result to be achieved from collaboration. On the other hand, greater pressure to increase the degree of internationalization could arise once firms have achieved a certain level of development in terms of managerial and organizational structure.

As far as the process of strategy formulation is concerned, in the case of the export consortia we investigated, their strategies were at least partially formalized. UNIDO consultants emphasized the importance of developing a business plan for the consortium in order to help partners share ideas about the mission and future of the network. Business planning can be a very useful activity for building consensus among partners, clarifying the basic business idea of the venture and identifying gaps and financial requirements. Therefore, even though consortia supported by UNIDO in developing countries generally consist of small firms, the need to enhance cohesion and commitment by participants motivated them to formulate an explicit strategy.

The formulation of a strategy is followed by its implementation: '*strategy formulation is the process of deciding what to do; strategy implementation is the process of performing all the activities necessary to do what has been planned*' (Carpenter and Sanders 2008: 12). However, formulation and implementation are highly interrelated.

The strategic planning process generally focuses on the following steps (Fig. 5.6): setting goals, developing a business idea, planning action, implementing strategy, assessing results and identifying any critical strategic issues. If there is an explicitly formulated strategy, it is good practice to assess actual results and compare them with the formulated goals and objectives. Any differences arising from this comparison are important in deciding whether to confirm or redefine the existing strategy. They can also be used to identify any critical network issues that require the setting of new goals and the updating or total reformulation of the strategy.

In the case of SME consortia, the output of strategy formulation is not a strategic plan *strictu sensu*, but rather an action plan or set of action plans. The main contents

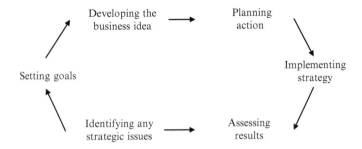

Fig. 5.6 The strategic planning process

of an action plans are: specific objectives; actions necessary to achieve them; the timing of each action; resources to be used and/or invested.

5.4 Designing the Organizational Structure

The organizational structure is the framework that management adopts in order to divide tasks and responsibilities, deploy resources and coordinate the activities and decisions of employees. The organizational structure of an export consortium must be designed on two levels:
1. The first step is to define the *macro-structure* by identifying the activities to be carried out by the consortium and those that will continue to be performed by member firms. This defines the organizational boundaries of the consortium;
2. The second is to design its *micro-structure* by identifying consortium organizational units and their roles, tasks and responsibilities.

These two elements merit separate analysis. The shape of the *macro-structure* reflects the rationale underlying the interfirm collaboration. As in any business network, the business activities of an export consortium may be allocated at two hierarchical levels, (a) member firm, (b) consortium. The design of the macro-structure is intended to define the organizational border between the two levels and define the activities to be carried out at each.

Export consortia may take different forms. When the partners are larger and more experienced, consortium strategy appears to be of minor concern and only ancillary to the autonomous internationalization strategies of the member firms. In other cases, the consortium strategy is of primary importance and designed to help member firms overcome the limitations associated with their resources and experience.

On the basis of the distinction between activities performed at consortium level and those which remain the responsibility of the member firms, three main models of consortium macro-structure can be identified: the *subsidiarity model*, the *model of strategic integration* and the *model of shared entrepreneurship* (Fig. 5.7). While these models are mutually exclusive, they may also represent evolutionary stages within any given consortium.

5.4 Designing the Organizational Structure

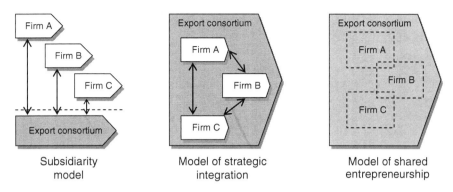

Fig. 5.7 Main forms of macro-structure for export consortia

The *subsidiarity model* is built on the rationale that strategic decisions are better taken at firm level. Member firms therefore dominate the strategy-making process; they continue to run their own businesses autonomously in the pursuit of individual goals, but share some common projects within the consortium. In this model, business at consortium level is mainly an additional activity; it represents a further opportunity for the entrepreneurs, but is not strictly necessary for the survival and growth of the firms. Interactions and linkages among member firms are minimal and there is little or no integration across their businesses. This is, for example, the case of *Mosaic*, where member firms are fairly independent, but share a number of activities aimed at increasing competitiveness. In such cases, investments by member firms are generally low and the consortium's tangible resources are very limited. Commitment is also limited. In fact, the composition of the consortium may change frequently as a result of firms joining or leaving the alliance based on their short-term economic convenience. Given the low investment on the part of member firms, fund-raising is crucial for the financing of consortium projects.

In the *Mosaic* consortium there are no common premises or dedicated offices as the consortium relies on the physical and managerial resources of its members (see Box 5.3). The organizational structure is light and has so far required little investment. The consortium's activities have been co-financed by national public institutions. The members of *Mosaic* are not yet oriented towards funding the development of the consortium entirely with their own resources. This is likely to be a key issue for the long-term success and survival of the network.

The *model of strategic integration* represents a more intense form of cooperation among firms, with a greater delegation of key activities to the consortium level, stronger network interactions and communications across partners, and a partial reduction in strategic autonomy at firm level. The consortium is not just an 'additional opportunity', but rather the beginning of a common framework within which member firms shape their strategies to achieve higher performance as a group. Synergies are more aggressively pursued and member firms share a number of business processes instead of acting independently. *Get'IT* is an example of a strategic integration macro-structure. Consistent with the intangible and virtual nature of its digital business, the consortium has a lean structure. The organization of specific promotional activities is outsourced to an external office that provides coordination and support services to *Get'IT*. The director of the consortium, who is elected by the entrepreneurs, is responsible for general management. There are no dedicated staff or professional managers, and the consortium has no assets of its own.

This model is usually adopted by firms which require more support for their internationalization strategy due to a lack of resources and competences. Commitment is generally higher compared to the previous model as the development of an effective model of integrated cooperation requires time and shared resources. In addition, the successful exploitation of synergies across partners makes it necessary to develop trust-based relationships in order to prevent opportunistic behaviours.

Finally, the *model of shared entrepreneurship* is the most involving and demanding organizational form of cooperation. In this model, all decisions concerning markets, products, processes and technologies are made and shared by the entrepreneurs, and all business activities are allocated on the basis of each firm's competences. The consortium becomes a highly-coordinated network. Although proprietary borders still remain, the organizational boundaries between the firms tend to disappear. Member firms behave like different units of a single organization, rather than independent businesses. Being closely linked and fully integrated within the consortium framework, firms act on the market as a single player. Members may still be formally autonomous, but their value chains are integrated in order to pursue a shared competitive strategy, and the success of any individual firm depends entirely on that of the consortium.

Phyto Uruguay is an example of a shared entrepreneurship structure. Member firms are highly integrated and have developed a consortium business idea which is implemented as if they were a single firm. This is consistent with the nature of *Phyto Uruguay* as a sales consortium.

In contrast to the subsidiarity model, the relationship between consortium and member firms in this case is totally inverted in favour of the former. As the consortium becomes a common venture for all its members, both a single leadership and a single entrepreneurial vision are necessary. The requirements for this model are therefore the emergence of a strong and clear internal entrepreneurial leadership across partners and, consequently, the formulation of a common strategy.

Once an export consortium's macro-structure has been designed, the next step is to define its *micro-structure*. This basically involves formally dividing the tasks and responsibilities entrusted to the consortium among the different organizational units and establishing the rules for coordinating decisions. The micro-structure is generally illustrated by charts displaying the organizational units and divisions of the consortium, and their hierarchical relationships. The more extensive and challenging the tasks at consortium level, the greater the organizational complexity of its micro-structure.

As far as the design of the microstructure is concerned, there are two main options which correspond to the two extremes of a *continuum* – a 'light' or 'heavy' structure. In the first case, the consortium has no (or very little) organizational structure of its own in terms of staff and resources; all of the responsibilities and tasks are distributed among the member firms, as with the subsidiarity model. This is the case of *Peruvian Bio*, which is characterized by an extremely simple structure. Meetings of the board, for example, are held on the premises of one of the partner firms. A representative of this firm is also president of the consortium, and no investment has been made in hiring specialized personnel.

The 'heavy' structure lies at the opposite end of the *continuum* and corresponds to a strategic integration or shared entrepreneurship macro-structure. The consortium needs its own staff and resources in order to achieve a high degree of integration within the business activities of its member firms.

Export consortia of this kind usually have an articulated structure of business units, and hire their own executives and employees to whom responsibilities and decision-making powers are delegated. Their activities have a greater impact on member firms as a larger number of projects may be carried out. However, the successful implementation of this organizational solution requires a high level of commitment on the part of member firms. In the case of *Travel Partner*, for example, the consortium has adopted a collegiate management system, in which the main tasks have been divided among four operational commissions: (a) purchases (airline companies, suppliers, insurance companies, etc.); (b) communications; (c) human resources; (d) exhibitions and trade fairs. Each commission is at the service of all of the member firms, who consider the division of tasks to be one of the most important advantages of the consortium.

The case of *Mosaic* is particularly interesting, as the consortium is likely to experience a shift from a light structure to a heavier one (see Box 5.3).

> **Box 5.3: The Organizational Structure of *Mosaic***
> The promotional consortium *Mosaic,* which operates in Casablanca, consists of six medium-large (120–330 employees) textile and garment firms all of which have already accumulated some export experience. Almost all of their production is currently sold abroad and the firms have a good knowledge of the mechanisms of international trade. In many of the firms, sales staff are fluent in at least French and English, and in some cases also in other European languages. All of the member firms are run directly by their owners. Their products are highly complementary. The likelihood of internal conflicts among firms when approaching international markets is therefore very low.
>
> The organization of *Mosaic* reflects the characteristics of the *subsidiarity model:* investments in the development of the organizational structure have so far been very low and its micro-structure is still very light. There are no dedicated offices as the consortium relies on the physical assets and managerial resources of the member firms. In fact, all of the consortium functions are divided among different firms (see Fig. 5.8), and board meetings (currently once a month) are hosted by the firms in turn. This structure is extremely cost-efficient and is perceived by the member firms as highly beneficial. However, given the increasing workload due to the recent expansion of consortium

(continued)

activities (training, promotion, sales, sourcing, etc.), the consortium is now evaluating whether it needs a permanent structure. Four years on from its foundation, new organizational and managerial needs have emerged, showing that the consortium is approaching a new stage of its lifecycle, requiring a new macro-structure (more similar to the model of strategic integration) and, consequently, a heavier micro-structure. Such a change will probably also affect the consortium strategy.

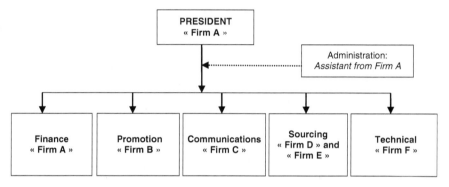

Fig. 5.8 The organizational structure of *Mosaic*

5.5 Leveraging on Strategic Resources and Competences

The results achieved by promotional or sales consortia are generally assessed in terms of marketing outcomes and sales. However, another important factor, although less evident, is the advantage that cooperation can bring in terms of development of new resources and competences for member firms.

All organizations – and consortia are no exception – need to consider the external environment when formulating strategy, but internal resources and capabilities are also key factors. Resource-based view researchers point out that firms are unique bundles of resources creating a competitive advantage (Wernerfelt 1984; Barney 1991). This set of firm-specific resources and competences drive the strategic behaviour of a firm and, therefore, its internationalization choices, which may be interpreted as how these resources and competences are exploited on a broader scale.

From this perspective, we can argue that a successful strategy can be pursued if the consortium has the tangible and intangible resources and competences which enable it to be competitive in its target markets. Given the consortium goals and objectives, the management needs to make decisions concerning the necessary resources and competences and subsequently identify those which the partners can provide, those which are to be internally developed, and those which need to

5.5 Leveraging on Strategic Resources and Competences

Table 5.1 A tool for assessing the contributions and needs of a consortium in terms of resources

Necessary resources	Resources possessed by member firms					Resources to be internally developed	Resources to be acquired from outside the consortium
	Partner A	Partner B	Partner C	Partner D	Partner E		
General management skills							
Marketing competences							
Sales and distribution competences							
Contacts with customers							
Productive competences							
Relationships with suppliers							
Financial resources							
Project management skills							

be acquired externally. Problems in the management of a consortium may arise if the partners make different contributions in terms of resources, resulting in an imbalance among partners that may generate excessive tension within the alliance.

Table 5.1 presents a tool for mapping the contributions of partner firms, in terms of resources and competences, and identifying the resource gaps which need to be filled in order to increase the chances of survival and growth of the consortium. This tool is also useful in assessing any imbalance between the resources provided by different member firms.

Firstly, the resources and competences necessary to carry out consortium activities and implement its strategy successfully need to be identified. These may include financial resources, marketing and management competences, relationships with customers and suppliers, technical assets and productive competences. Resources and competences may fall into three categories: resources possessed by member firms; resources to be internally developed; resources to be acquired from outside the consortium. For resources and competences already possessed by member firms, the strategic issue is mainly to enhance the transfer and mutual exchange between partners in order to strengthen the resource base of the consortium as a whole. Other resources and competences may be developed and upgraded through a number of activities and projects carried out directly by the consortium. For example, training activities expand and improve competences in areas such as human resource management, productive processes or procurement activities. Finally, there may be strategic resources which need to be acquired from outside the consortium. For example, given the lack of professional managers, an export consortium may decide to appoint an external general manager.

Resources are what a firm uses to create goods or services, and can range from physical and tangible, to intangible and knowledge-based (Grant 1991). They are used to create inimitable capabilities (Amit and Schoemaker 1993; Dierickx and Cool 1989). Competences and capabilities refer to a firm's skill in using its resources, and derive from the experience and expertise of employees or the procedures embedded in a firm's routines.

The importance of resources and capabilities lies in the fact that not all competitors have access to the same resources and competences, and not all resources or competences enable a firm to develop a sustainable competitive advantage. Barney (1991) developed the VRINE model for analysing a firm's resources and how they relate to competitive advantage. The VRINE model suggests that a firm can create competitive advantage by leveraging on resources and capabilities that are:
- valuable in allowing the firm to seize opportunities or reduce threats;
- rare, given that the more limited or exclusive access to a resource is, the greater the advantage in possessing it;
- inimitable, insofar as they either cannot be acquired by competitors, or the cost of acquisition is too high;
- non-substitutable, meaning that the benefit related to possession cannot be obtained by a competitor using a different resource or combination of resources;
- exploitable, because controlling a resource or capability does not result in any competitive advantage unless it can be exploited, i.e. turned into value.

Tangible resources can easily be imitated or replaced and are therefore less likely to be a source of competitive advantage than intangible resources such as knowledge, reputation, organizational culture and marketing skills. In particular, intangible resources are strategic for the internationalization process, as the pursuit of growth strategies at international level makes it necessary to develop and deploy different and more sophisticated resources than those required at domestic level. Greater knowledge of foreign markets, higher market reputation, relational capabilities needed to develop business contacts abroad, and management skills needed to handle the greater complexity associated with foreign operations are examples of resources and capabilities that firms need to enhance in order to be successful in foreign markets.

One important factor in a firm's available resources is the network of relation ships in which it is embedded. A number of studies have focused on the use of networks by SMEs in pursuing international opportunities (Chetty and Agndal 2007; Chetty and Holm 2000; Coviello 2006). By working more closely together, firms can access, combine and share expertise, resources and knowledge, and co-produce additional knowledge in ways which would be impossible by acting independently. This is especially true of SMEs, which generally lack the resources and competences needed to be competitive in a global environment.

Networking is increasingly seen primarily as a means of acquiring resources. The importance of networks for SMEs is also due to the learning outcomes that come from participation in networks. SMEs not only learn *from* their partners (by accessing and acquiring the partners' knowledge and competences), but also *with* their partners, by developing new collective competences and resources as a result of the interactions which their common participation in the consortium implies.

> **Box 5.4: The Resources Gathered and Developed by *Get'IT***
> The Tunisian consortium *Get'IT* consists of 11 ICT firms. Joining the consortium developed into an opportunity for these firms to leverage on a number of resources and competences which they would have been unable to develop alone. Participation in the consortium provided access to additional financial resources, especially from FAMEX (National Fund for Access to Export Markets) and, recently, also from FODEC (Fund for Development of Competitiveness), for their internationalization process. Many of the consortium activities are co-financed by FAMEX (up to 70% of all eligible costs), and public funds represent between 40% and 60% of the consortium budget. This has been a significant benefit for member firms as these funds would not have been available without the consortium. Furthermore, the consortium contribution, in terms of resource development for member firms, is mainly in the field of intangible resources, particularly knowledge, relational capital and image. As perceived by its members, the benefits of belonging to the consortium largely consist of access to greater knowledge of international markets and 'relational' capital, including business contacts, business partnerships, and agency contracts with fundamental ICT providers. In addition, and in line with the strategic objective of 'enriching the offer through complementary and diversified ICT solutions', one of the main achievements of the consortium's first years of activity has been the construction of a clearly recognized and highly visible brand and image. Many of its customers in Tunisia and abroad acknowledge *Get'IT* as an ICT partnership offering a wide range of competences and qualified human resources.

Empirical evidence on export consortia promoted by UNIDO in developing countries shows that the contribution of the consortia in the development of the firms' resources is particularly important in the area of intangible resources, which play a fundamental role as sources of competitive advantage.

Table 5.2 summarizes the main activities carried out by the export consortia in order to develop intangible resources for internationalization. We have classified resources into four categories: information, relationships, know-how and image/reputation. These categories are not exhaustive. The literature on resources has proposed several broader classifications (Grant 1991; Hall 1993). However, the classification below is preferred as empirical investigation has shown these resources to be particularly relevant to the analysis of export consortia and therefore better suited to the research setting of our study.

In all nine cases, the consortia contributed to the enhancement of reputation at both firm- and consortium-level. The development of a 'common identity' is

Table 5.2 Intangible resources developed by UNIDO consortia

	Information	Relationships	Know-how	Image and reputation
Mosaic	Creation of a shared database of customers and suppliers	Development of business contacts abroad through participation in fairs and trade missions	Enhancement of technical competences On-the-job training activities for employees of member firms	Creation of the consortium brand and shared image (website, logo, brochure). Increased reputation of firms
Vitargan	–	Development of business contacts abroad through participation in fairs and trade missions	Enhancement of technical and marketing competences due to training activities Increase in firms' procurement competences Attainment of the internationally recognised ECOCERT BIO certification	Development of a stronger and shared image owing to common marketing and communication activities
Travel partners	Enhanced knowledge transfer among partners about markets and suppliers	Access to new markets through commercial missions	Development of competences in the areas of procurement and human resources management via training activities	Enhancement of firms' common unique image and external communication (website, logo, catalogue) Higher visibility of member firms on national markets
Get'It	Development of a shared and integrated CRM (Customer Relationship Management) system	Participation in specialized ICT Forums Development of business contacts with the main international ICT providers	–	Development of the consortium brand and communication Higher visibility of member firms on national markets
Muyu	Creation of a shared database of customers and suppliers	–	Training activities for entrepreneurs and employees in the areas of strategic planning, communication, sales techniques, design, and technology	Development of the firms' common logo, website and promotional materials (CD-ROMs and catalogue) for foreign distributors

(continued)

5.5 Leveraging on Strategic Resources and Competences 103

Table 5.2 (continued)

	Information	Relationships	Know-how	Image and reputation
Peruvian Bio Consortia	–	Development of business contacts abroad through participation in fairs and trade missions	Enhancement of technical and marketing competences	Development of the firms' common identity (consortium logo, mission and vision) and external communication (consortium's website, promotional materials and advertising)
ACMC	–	Development of contacts with other networks of SMEs within the country Development of contacts with national public organizations	–	Creation of the consortium brand and development of the firms' common identity (website, logo)
Ande Natura	Exchange of information on partners and suppliers	Development of business contacts abroad through participation in fairs and trade missions Stronger relationships with national private and public institutions	Enhancement of technical and marketing competences	Development of the consortium image (website, promotional CD-ROM) and brand
Phyto Uruguay	–	Development of business contacts and new national and international contracts	Ethical and environmental certification	Development of a shared brand for products of all firms Communication activities at consortium level

generally highlighted by member firms as an important result achieved due to the following activities of the consortia: creation of a logo or consortium brand (fundamental for the development of an integrated offer to the market), creation of the consortium website, development of common promotional materials (such as brochures and CD-ROMs) and a number of jointly implemented marketing actions. In a small number of cases, activities also included publication of a catalogue of consortium products and advertising in specialist magazines. In addition, two consortia – *Vitargan* and *Phyto Uruguay* – obtained important environmental certification which contributed to increasing the reputation of member firms in both domestic and international markets. Such certification is much more significant when we consider that firms would have been unable to obtain it by acting individually.

'Relations' and 'know-how' are two important areas where the contribution of the consortia has proved important. In almost all cases consortia have assisted member firms in establishing business contacts with potential customers, in both domestic and international markets. The development of 'relational capital' not only refers to relationships with customers, but also with public and private institutions, which are central to the acquisition of financial resources. As far as 'know-how' is concerned, a greater knowledge of foreign markets and the enhancement of marketing capabilities are two important achievements of the consortia. However, the competences of member firms have also been upgraded in other areas as a result of consortium participation. These include production and procurement activities and human resource management. Training activities for entrepreneurs and employees have favoured this process of competence upgrading.

Finally, in five of the consortia, valuable results have been reported regarding creation of databases of suppliers, customers, and competitors. Within the category 'information', we can also include the benefits for member firms in terms of information and knowledge flow concerning markets, customers, and suppliers.

The empirical analysis also allowed us to shed light on the operation of the consortia from a dynamic point of view. When consortium strategy is analyzed, a common pattern emerges from the different case studies particularly regarding the development of intangible resources.

Basically, the creation of new strategic resources starts with three actions, which may be considered milestones in every export consortium strategy: the development of relationships with national institutions, the organization of trade missions and fairs abroad and the enhancement of collaboration within the network itself, i.e. among member firms. These actions fuel a process that links consortium strategy to the generation of strategic resources for member firms, as shown in Fig. 5.9.

The *development of relationships with national institutions* (a) is fundamental not only for building consensus and supporting consortium strategy, but also because it allows the acquisition of those *financial resources* (d) which generally represent a major source of public funding for the international development of member firms. In all cases, this source co-finances over 50% of the costs of all consortium projects. Financial resources are needed by the small firms in order to develop an *effective consortium image, brand and communication policy* (h) and carry out *training programmes for executives and employees* of the firms (i), thus developing new *technical and managerial know-how* inside the consortium (l). Finally, these financial resources are used by the consortia to finance (or co-finance) the *commercial missions of the entrepreneurs or sales managers to foreign markets and participation in trade fairs abroad* (b).

Participation in missions and fairs abroad feeds the *database of information about potential new customers* for the member firms (e) (which is a sound

5.5 Leveraging on Strategic Resources and Competences

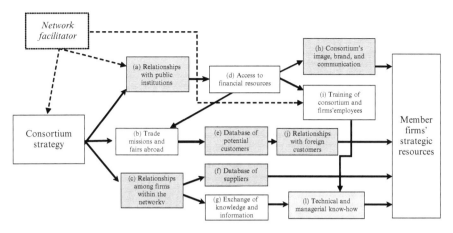

Fig. 5.9 The role of export consortia in the development of intangible resources for internationalization: a dynamic view

strategic resource for every export consortium), as well as fostering the generation of business contacts and *relations with foreign prospects or customers* (j). Databases of customers and suppliers and, in general, market knowledge and business contacts are among the most valuable tools for the development plans of an export consortium.

Finally, the investment of export consortia in the development of relationships is aimed not only towards external actors, but also has a positive effect on the *enhancement of collaboration among the firms* (c) that constitute the strategic network. Our cases show that among member firms an extensive and significant detailed *exchange of knowledge and information* (g) occurs which, in turn, encourages the acquisition and dissemination of *technical and managerial know-how* (l).

The grey boxes in Fig. 5.9 show the range of resources which make up the final set of intangible resources at member firm level. They are concentrated mainly in the area of so-called 'relational capital'. In particular, relationships are crucial not only between member firms, but also outside them, i.e. in terms of links with public institutions. In addition, with regard to the development of these intangible resources within the export consortia, the importance of UNIDO as a 'network facilitator' clearly emerges in the cases covered by our empirical analysis. It is worth noting that the role played by UNIDO goes far beyond supporting the initiatives of individual member firms. It is crucially important in all stages of the consortia life cycle, from the selection of member firms to the setting-up of the organizational structure and governance mechanisms. Furthermore, UNIDO, in its role as network facilitator, has supported the consortia in building their own relationships on foreign markets and fostered collaboration between the consortia and the public institutions which finance most of the consortia activities.

5.6 Enforcing Corporate Governance and Leadership

The governance structure of the consortium greatly affects the strategic alignment of member firms and their commitment. Like any other interfirm network, export consortia are 'multi-stakeholder' organizations where the interests of a variety of actors come together. Each of these actors holds a specific stake in the life of the organization. Member firms expect their particular interests to be kept under careful consideration by the consortium. The concept of stakeholder is therefore at the core of corporate governance (Freeman 1984). In the case of export consortia, the member firms are the primary stakeholders. They play a fundamental role in influencing overall performance and achieving strategic goals.

In management studies, the narrow sense of the term 'corporate governance' refers to the set of choices regarding the configuration and modes of functioning of a firm's steering body. The design of the governance structure responds to the following questions: Who in the consortium has the right to make strategic decisions (all of the partners, the board of directors or a general manager)? Who assumes leadership of the network at the different stages of the consortium's lifecycle (the President of the board, a general manager or an external broker/facilitator)? What rules does the decision-making process follow? What are the criteria for the admission of new partners? And what are the mechanisms for sharing costs and benefits among member firms?

In a broader sense, the term 'corporate governance' refers to all activities aimed at defining the organization's goals and the sharing of those goals among stakeholders. From this perspective, governance issues concern the composition and functioning of governance bodies, the management of internal and external communication and, more generally, the management of the relationships with the organization's stakeholders (Bain and Band 1996; Kendall and Kendall 1998).

Corporate governance strongly impacts on the strategic management of an export consortium. This is because defining the governance system implies (a) designing effective top-level management bodies, (b) ensuring real participation of each member firm in the strategy-making process, (c) communicating clearly to these primary stakeholders the objectives, strategies and performance of the consortium, (d) guaranteeing control of member firms over all decisions and actions implemented by the consortium and, finally, (e) putting systems in place to monitor and measure customer satisfaction and participation.

Top-level management bodies are assumed to be responsible for an extremely important set of tasks (Mintzberg 1983). These include analyzing and monitoring the environment in which the consortium operates, formulating the consortium strategy, allocating collective resources to the different programmes carried out by the consortium, assessing the alignment between organizational design and strategy, managing the consortium staff, representing the consortium in its relationship with internal and external stakeholders.

In export consortia, carrying out these tasks necessarily requires an effective involvement of member firms. At every stage of the consortium's life, all members must be involved in the decision-making process and are expected to participate

5.6 Enforcing Corporate Governance and Leadership

directly in top-level management bodies. In the very early stages and, generally, when consortium activities are not very significant compared to the business of individual firms, the simplest way to guarantee participation is to involve all the entrepreneurs in the board of directors. As the network grows and the number of partners increases, leaner and more effective governance bodies, such as an elected board of directors, become the *locus* where strategic decisions are made. In elected boards, given that some member firms are not represented, the adoption of a formal set of rules about the decision-making process and the development of monitoring systems become fundamental in order to guarantee the interests of the individual firms.

If the consortium develops a set of business activities independent from those of the individual firms, it becomes necessary to delegate some decision-making power to one or more managers. The consortium can choose different solutions, ranging from a governance structure where the board continues to be the strategic leader of the consortium, to one where a general manager emerges as strategic leader. These two alternatives have different effects on the functioning and power equilibrium of the consortium.

In the first case, the consortium may decide to keep the strategic leadership internal, confirming the role of this collective body as a 'strong one'. This is possible if the board has a lean structure and if there is a shared entrepreneurial vision. In those consortia where the board is very large, it is possible to create a more restricted inner collective body, usually known as a 'steering committee', in order to streamline the decision-making process. This choice is usually designed to avoid the inefficiencies and delays which are typical of oversized decision-making bodies. The steering committee is normally chaired by the consortium's president and is composed of a restricted number of executives appointed by the board. The general manager of the consortium (if such a position exists) also participates, though without voting rights. The board can delegate to the steering committee a major part of the day-to-day management, which is usually performed jointly by all members. Alternatively, the consortium can opt for a structure where the board delegates part of its power to a general manager who takes on the strategic leadership (under the board's control). This is the case of the 'managerial model', which is centred on the general manager figure. The board appoints the general manager, who then selects the management team.

The appointment of a general manager is an important decision related to the governance structure of the consortium. Most of the export consortia included in our empirical analysis do not have a general manager, mainly due to their small size and limited time in operation. However, in some cases, the need to introduce a professional manager at the top of the consortium structure is now emerging as a consequence of the development of consortia activities. In 2007, for example, the Moroccan consortium *Travel Partner* hired a temporary general manager (coordinator), charged with organizing weekly meetings and implementing the actions provided for in the action plan. In *Muyu,* on the other hand, leadership has been taken on by one of the partner entrepreneurs. She was selected by the others owing to her experience in both the industry and in export activities (see Box 5.5).

The consortium general manager plays a pivotal role in the management of the network, especially when member firms are not particularly active (Depperu 1996).

In the start-up phase the consortium manager is responsible for setting up meetings, pooling resources and developing ideas for the first steps of the network activity. Consequently, this role is crucial for implementing the network strategy, coordinating the activities of member firms, and resolving problems related to conflicts between partners.

The success of an export consortium depends largely on the trust that members develop towards the consortium manager (Welch et al. 1996). Moreover, the greater the complexity of the activities of the consortium, the greater the need for highly professional managers. When a general manager is present, the board remains formally the supreme governing body, entitled to steer the consortium. However, the ability of this governing body to substantially influence the decision-making process will depend on how the relationship between the board and the general manager develops. The most frequent outcome is a power division of sorts between the two organs: the board is specifically committed to the planning of all institutional activities related to the consortium's mission; the general manager is responsible for all technical, productive, administrative and organizational activities. When managers with significant decision-making power are present, the role of the board is less operational, focusing mostly on the definition of goals and the long-term strategy of the consortium. The board/manager dual structure works well when both the respective roles and the extent of the general manager's powers are well defined. Otherwise, there is a potential for conflict.

Beyond the design of governing bodies, the definition of the rules concerning relationships between partners is a critical activity. Research on both successful and unsuccessful alliances shows that precise definition of partners' rights and duties is a highly relevant factor to the success of alliances (Hoffman and Schlosser 2001). The application of this concept may result in very simple rules. *Ande Natura*, for example, has adopted a rule whereby partners are fined for missing meetings.

Another important question is the definition of criteria for admission and expulsion of partners. At the very outset of consortium activities the circumstances in which a new partner may be admitted and the rules for decisions concerning admissions must be clearly defined. Procedures for dealing with the exit of partners must also be decided upon during the start-up phase. This is necessary in order to prevent conflicts among members.

Cost-sharing mechanisms are another key issue. Some activities can only be implemented efficiently if a high number of firms are involved. Other activities can be successfully carried out even though a limited number of partners contribute to covering costs. It is therefore necessary to set clear and simple rules which regulate the participation of firms in consortium activities.

The need to guarantee each member a fair and satisfactory balance between investment (in terms of both financial and human contributions) and benefit can be met through applying flexible mechanisms. In the case of *Vitargan*, member firms share the costs of the activities in which they participate, covering 25%. The other 75% is financed by an EU support programme. *Get'IT's* operating costs, on the other hand, are covered by its member firms, who pay a fixed amount, while there are additional specific contributions to the costs of individual activities. In the

Mosaic consortium, each enterprise can choose whether or not to participate in a given activity, and the consortium does not require a fixed annual contribution. Each activity is equally financed by the participating member firms only, and usually also benefits from public co-financing. *Mosaic* has thus embraced a sort of 'variable geometry' paradigm based on the idea that not every firm needs to take part in every activity, and partners can cooperate to varying degrees in the different projects.

In addition, whenever consortia are launched with support from an external agency, one crucial decision is when to withdraw from active involvement (Welch et al. 1998). Identifying the appropriate time to withdraw is problematic, as it is not always clear when a group is capable of proceeding successfully without support. Control which is too rigid, on the other hand, may have the effect of breaking the informal links between partners. In fact, a high level of dependence on the facilitator may represent a risk to the success of the consortium.

The experience of UNIDO appears to have been very positive as far as project development and the start-up phase are concerned. As discussed in previous chapters, UNIDO played a key role as 'network facilitator'. As Welch et al. (1998: 72) maintain: '*A government trade promotion agency, as an honest broker, has legitimacy, whereas a group member is likely to find it difficult to organise and host such activities because of a perceived vested interest, especially if the group includes competitors*'. UNIDO support has also been crucial in securing financial aid from public institutions. The extent to which the consortia will be able to continue developing their activities when such support ends is still a 'question mark,' as this phase has not yet been experienced.

Finally, in order to ensure that the governance system effectively satisfies member firms, it is necessary to monitor their participation and satisfaction through continuously assessing the cost-benefit balance.

Box 5.5: The Governance System of *Muyu* The export consortium *Muyu* was founded in 2005. It is currently composed of five micro and small handicraft firms from Cusco, Peru. They all manufacture and sell handmade products based on Peruvian tradition. The launch of the consortium was preceded by a period of informal cooperation among members. Initially, this cooperation involved a larger number of members, namely a group of ten small Peruvian firms that recently participated in a publicly-funded aid programme for artisans. Subsequently, seven of them formed a network of firms, made possible by a special support programme of the Peruvian Ministry of Labour, and began to concentrate their promotional activities on the US and European markets. Finally, in 2005, six of these firms decided to found the *Muyu* consortium, which, one year later, was formally converted into an export consortium, supported by UNIDO. Soon after, however, in 2007, one of the founding members decided to leave the consortium, due to a disagreement with the other partners over the division of costs and revenues in one of the projects set up by the consortium. As a result, there are now five members.

(continued)

The exit of five member firms at different stages of the life of the alliance may be traced back to two fundamental causes: firstly, a lack of trust among some members and secondly, the conflicts among member firms arising from their differing visions of the strategy and governance of the network. According to the current members of *Muyu*, these two problem areas have been definitively resolved. The level of trust among members has progressively increased and gradually reinforced as a result of the successful implementation of numerous consortium activities during the first three years. Furthermore, the consortium has formalized its strategy, formulated its mission and identified the strategic objectives, at both consortium and firm level. A formal set of rules has been adopted in order to regulate the functioning of the consortium and the relationships among members, and to prevent conflicts. Strategic alignment is also ensured by selection criteria of members: All members are expected to have a certain degree of export experience and to offer products with quality standards that meet the requirements of export markets.

The consortium is now managed by a steering committee, composed of three people. One entrepreneur serves as coordinator; she was selected by the others for her extensive experience in export, good knowledge of handicraft markets, and public relations ability. A second entrepreneur holds the post of treasurer. Finally, there is an externally recruited general manager, independent of the member firms. Two key elements therefore characterize the structure of this consortium: the presence of a strong leader and a professional manager, even though only on a part-time basis. The governance of the consortium ensures the full participation of all the members in the strategic decisions. The five entrepreneurs meet twice a month, using the offices of each member firm in turn. This rotation in the hosting of consortium meetings encourages visits to the headquarters of the other partners. In general, there are no restrictions to visiting the offices of the other firms. As a result there is open and frequent communication and information exchange among the firms. The consortium has worked effectively during its first three years of activity due to the high level commitment and participation of the member firms, thus enhancing the trust-based relationships between the partners. This mutual trust has also been indirectly fostered by the high complementarity of the firms' products, dramatically reducing potential sources of conflict and making the synergy of cooperation evident.

The issue of balance between contributions and benefits has also been effectively addressed. Currently, all the financial resources of the consortium are provided by the member firms. They all contribute to the consortium's budget in two ways: firstly, through a fixed and equal annual sum, used to cover the operating costs of the consortium and secondly, with additional contributions for the funding of specific activities or projects, such as participation in fairs. In this second case, contributions to cover costs are made only by those partners involved in the projects.

5.7 Measuring Consortium Performance

Firms join a consortium to exploit synergies and achieve goals that they would not be able to achieve individually. The starting point for evaluating the success of a consortium is to assess the balance *over time* between the *contributions* made by firms and the *benefits* they receive. A firm's reason for participating in a consortium is a function of the perceived 'net balance' between the sum of all the advantages or expected benefits, and the costs that such participation entails.

In a broad perspective, an analysis of consortium performance should include the level of the member firms' *participation, commitment, and benefits/satisfaction*. *Participation* may be measured by the number of activities/projects in which a firm has taken part in relation to the total number of projects carried out in a given period of time. *Commitment* is associated with the financial and human resources that a firm has invested in order to co-finance consortium initiatives. *Benefits* refer to the overall level of satisfaction of the firm in terms of achieving expected results.

This analysis should also take into account the differences between sales and promotional consortia. The key strategic objective of a promotional consortium is to involve its partners in promotional activities and projects. There is no direct relationship between a promotional consortium and external customers, as its services are mainly directed at its own members. These consortia therefore do not have sales of their own, and so performance is closely related to the level of member firms' participation in consortium activities.

Measuring the performance of an export consortium is not quite as straightforward. Mere survival is often used as a measure of success (Welch et al. 1996, 1998). The number of years a firm has belonged to a consortium may be used as a proxy for its commitment to the consortium strategy. However, it does not in itself indicate success or commitment. One firm may belong to a consortium for an extended period but obtain poor results due to a lack of involvement, whereas another may participate very actively for a shorter period of time, and then decide to leave the network when it considers it has fully achieved the objectives which formed the basis of its participation.

Analysing the benefits which a firm obtains from consortium membership involves considering a number of factors, especially in the case of sales consortia. Performance is a multi-dimensional construct, and research suggests it is best examined in both financial and market/operational terms. In a broader sense, the benefits obtained and the satisfaction of member firms may be divided into six areas (Fig. 5.10):

– *Financial outcomes* are usually assessed using accounting-based measures. In the *Vitargan* case, for example, a significant improvement in profits has been achieved as a result of lower purchasing costs after member firms decided to carry out their purchasing activities jointly. This decision resulted in a much higher bargaining power than when negotiating individually.
– *Market outcomes* may be measured by looking at export sales and trends over time (export growth), the number of new countries served, and other marketing

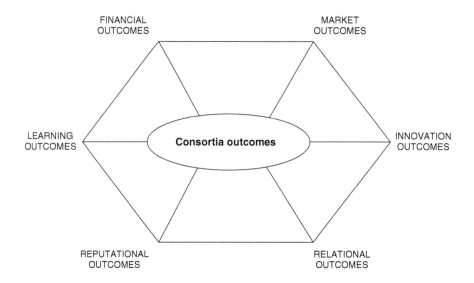

Fig. 5.10 Consortia outcomes

benefits. *Travel Partner* members, for example, have obtained three main market advantages by leveraging on cooperation: stronger common image/identity, greater visibility on the national market and access to new markets, in the form of both new countries and untapped niche markets.
- *Learning outcomes* refer to the benefits arising from a firm's acquisition and development of knowledge-based resources and competences *from* and *with* the other partners. All the managers of the travel agencies which make up *Travel Partner* agree that being part of the consortium has provided a new strategic channel for the exchange of information and knowledge, resulting in a greater capacity to compete in foreign markets.
- *Reputational outcomes* relate to the increase in brand recognition of the individual members and the consortium as a whole, and is particularly relevant in promotional consortia. In many cases, joining a consortium allows member firms to adopt a common brand, which generally enhances their marketing capability. However, this is not the only example of a reputational outcome. In the case of *Phyto Uruguay,* an important result for all the firms has been the securing of international certifications such as ISO 9001 and GMP – Good Manufacturing Practice. GMP is a globally recognized certification for the control and management of the production and quality control testing of foodstuffs and pharmaceutical products.
- *Innovation outcomes*: firms receive important inputs which enable them to upgrade and innovate their range of products and services as a result of consortium participation. In some cases, firms need to redefine their value proposition in order to achieve greater strategic alignment with one another and create a more homogeneous consortium offer. The case of *Phyto Uruguay*, for example,

demonstrates that almost all of the consortium partners have reviewed their products, packaging and promotional material, and the majority have invested in new equipment and technologies as a consequence of entering the alliance.
– *Relational outcomes* are a highly significant aspect of consortium success. Consortia aim to assist firms in developing new business contacts at home and abroad. It can be useful, therefore, to measure satisfaction in terms of number and quality of the business relationships developed via the network.

The *Mosaic* consortium provides a good example of the multiple benefits associated with participation in a consortium. Member firms have benefited from a number of advantages which may be summarized as follows:
– Participation in new fairs as well as more successful participation in traditional fairs due to higher visibility and better image of firms.
– The setting-up of a shared database of suppliers and clients.
– Higher bargaining power towards suppliers, in terms of: lower fees and prices (as compared to individual companies) for participation in fairs and trade missions, export insurance and the purchase of other goods and services.
– Development of technological and market intelligence activities which cannot be performed by SMEs individually.
– Mutual coaching and information exchange aimed at solving common problems.
– Establishment of action plans for both the consortium and member firms with UNIDO support.
– The move from subcontracting to co-contracting through the establishment of a product development department.
– Higher profitability of export activities (though difficult to measure).

The implementation of the performance measurement system builds on the assessment of the impact of the activities performed by the consortium on achieving its strategic objectives. On the basis of the consortium objectives, it is possible to develop a system of key performance indicators (KPIs) for the consortium as a whole, as well as for the individual firms, by defining a set of items that reasonably approximate the performance dimensions described above (Fig. 5.11).

KPIs must be measurable. Performance may be measured using either objective measures – such as considering sales trends, percentage of sales due to exports, profitability – or subjective measures, such as the firms' perceived degree of satisfaction with consortium activities and the degree of participation of member firms in consortium initiatives. The use of self-reported performance measurements is quite common in SME research (Cavusgil and Zou 1994; Shoham 1998; Zou and Stan 1998). In fact, profitability and other aspects of financial performance do not provide complete information about internationalization, especially in the case of SMEs where accounting measures tend to be less reliable than in larger firms, and financial performance does not necessarily reflect success (Kotey and Meredith 1997).

Figure 5.11 presents some examples of possible KPIs related to the different objectives of an export consortium. It is also necessary to take into account the difficulties of isolating the effect of consortium membership on performance. In order to evaluate the extent to which a firm's participation in the consortium has

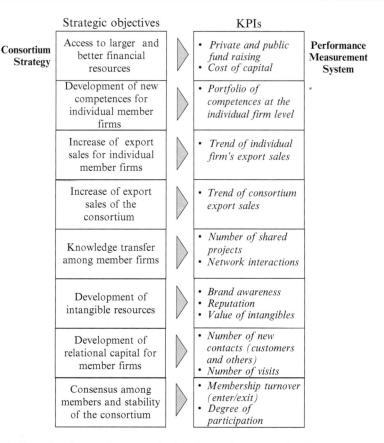

Fig. 5.11 Examples of consortium strategic objectives and corresponding KPIs

made it possible to obtain greater benefits than those a firm could have achieved alone, it may be necessary to rely on the perceptions of the managers. For example, it is almost impossible to isolate the effect of participating in the consortium on an individual firm's sales. Therefore, the trend of export sales could be integrated via a subjective estimation of the 'consortium effect' on export performance by asking the firms to rate the extent to which they consider their export sales as depending on consortium activities (e.g. by using a 5-point Likert scale in which 1 indicates 'not at all' and 5 'to a great extent').

An example of an analytical tool for assessing each initiative promoted by the consortium is shown in Table 5.3. Each action or project is identified by a label and classified as either a collective, 'core' activity involving all of the member firms (C) or a voluntary activity (V). As shown in the table, various data should be collected for each activity (budget, amount of public funding, names of participating firms, level of perceived satisfaction). In order to assess the benefits associated with the initiative, entrepreneurs could be asked to rate their level of satisfaction in terms of

5.7 Measuring Consortium Performance

Table 5.3 Overview of activities carried out by the consortium

Activity	Type of activity	Start date (mm/yy)	Budget (US$)	Public funding (%)	Firm A	Firm B	Firm C	Firm ...	Average level of satisfaction (%)
					\multicolumn{4}{c}{Names of participating firms}	
1.									
2.									
3.									
4.									
5.									
...									

Table 5.4 A tool for measuring the contribution of the consortium to the enhancement of member firms' resources and competences

Since our firm joined the consortium	Decreased	Remained the same	Slightly increased	Increased	Greatly increased
Our marketing competences have...					
Our administrative competences have...					
Our technical competences have...					
Our knowledge of foreign markets and customers has...					
The number of our customers abroad has...					
The number of our business contacts abroad has...					
The number of business proposals presented to potential new international customers last year...					
Our reputation and visibility have...					

achievement of their initial objectives. Responses could be measured as either a percentage (assuming 100% as total satisfaction) or through the use of 5- or 7-point Likert scales. In this way we would be able to measure the success of the consortium in terms of average score for each initiative, overall satisfaction of the firm for both individual activities and global capacity of the consortium to satisfy the needs of member firms over time.

Perceptual measures could also be adopted to assess the benefits from participation in the consortium in terms of the enhancement of individual firms' resources and capabilities (Table 5.4). Similarly, such measures could also assess improvements in the 'relational capital' and enlargement of the business network (suppliers, customers and business contacts in general) in which the firm is embedded as a result of its participation in the consortium.

> **Box 5.6: Monitoring the Performance of the *Muyu* Consortium**
> The performance of the Peruvian consortium *Muyu* was monitored from 2005 to 2007 by applying a multidimensional system of measures including: revenues and exports, employment, participation in consortium activities, degree of members' satisfaction with the achievement of original objectives and development of new resources. The assumption behind the adoption of this system is that no single measure can provide a comprehensive representation of consortium success; only an integrated analysis allows for a global assessment. Since its foundation in 2005, *Muyu* has undertaken a large number of initiatives, and their impact is assessed at both firm and consortium level. The trends of the commercial results of the individual firms in terms of revenues and percentage of export sales are monitored, although it is evident that changes in revenues and export cannot be considered a direct result of the consortium's activities. In fact, performance also depends largely on competitive and environmental factors as well as the strategies and actions of the individual firms. For example, one of the member firms reported negative performance mainly due to the crisis affecting its industry during the period 2005–2007. The achievements of the consortium are also considered to include the increase in the number of employees, which can be attributed indirectly to the promotional activities of the consortium. Specifically, two of the five member firms increased their employee numbers over the 2005–2007 period.
>
> The achievement of *Muyu*'s strategic objectives as perceived by member firms is reported in Table 5.5

Table 5.5 Member firms' perception of *Muyu*'s achievement of targets (%)

Consortium strategic objectives	Firm 'A'	Firm 'B'	Firm 'C'	Firm 'D'	Firm 'E'	Average (%)
To increase member firms' competitiveness	70	80	70	60	80	72
To gain better positioning and market share in domestic and international markets	80	70	70	70	80	74
To position *Muyu* as a high quality brand	70	70	60	60	70	66
To plan product innovation	70	70	70	60	70	68
To increase productivity and standardize member firms' products	70	70	70	60	70	68
To develop managerial competences and tools	80	70	70	60	70	70

Achievement as perceived by member firms (100% as full achievement)

References

Amit, R., & Schoemaker, P. (1993). Strategic assets & organizational rent. *Strategic Management Journal, 14*(1), 33–46.

Bain, N., & Band, D. (1996). *Winning ways through corporate governance*. Houndmills/Hampshire: McMillan Business.

Barney, J. B. (1991). Firm resources and sustained competitive advantage. *Journal of Management, 17*(1), 99–120.

Carpenter, M. A., & Sanders, W. G. (2008). *Strategic management. A dynamic perspective*. Upper Saddle River: Prentice Hall.

Cavusgil, S. T., & Zou, S. (1994). Marketing strategy-performance relationship: An investigation of the empirical link in export market ventures. *Journal of Marketing, 58*(1), 1–21.

Chetty, S., & Agndal, H. (2007). Social capital and its influence on changes in internationalization mode among small and medium-sized enterprises. *Journal of International Marketing, 15*(1), 1–29.

Chetty, S., & Holm, D. B. (2000). Internationalisation of small to medium-sized manufacturing firms: A network approach. *International Business Review, 9*(1), 77–93.

Collins, J. C., & Porras, J. I. (1996). Building your company's vision. *Harvard Business Review*, September–October, 2–13.

Coviello, N. E. (2006). The network dynamics of international new ventures. *Journal of International Business Studies, 37*(5), 713–731.

Depperu, D. (1996). *Economia dei consorzi tra imprese*. Milano: Egea.

Dierickx, I., & Cool, K. (1989). Asset stock accumulation & sustainability of competitive. *Management Science, 35*(12), 1504–1511.

Freeman, R. E. (1984). *Strategic management: A stakeholder approach*. London: Pitman.

Grant, R. M. (1991). The resource-based theory of competitive advantage: Implications for strategy formulation. *California Management Review, 33*(3), 114–135.

Hall, R. (1993). A framework linking intangible resources and capabilities to sustainable competitive advantage. *Strategic Management Journal, 14*(8), 607–618.

Hax, A. C., & Majluf, N. S. (1991). *The strategy concept and process. A pragmatic approach*. Upper Saddle River: Prentice Hall.

Hoffman, W. H., & Schlosser, R. (2001). Success factors of strategic alliances in small and medium-sized enterprises – An empirical survey. *Long Range Planning, 34*(3), 354–381.

Kendall, N., & Kendall, A. (1998). *Real-world corporate governance*. London: Pitman.

Kotey, B., & Meredith, G. G. (1997). Relationships among owner and manager personal values, business strategies, and enterprise performance. *Journal of Small Business Management, 35*(2), 37–65.

McEvily, B., & Zaheer, A. (2004). Architects of trust: The role of network facilitators in geographical clusters. In R. M. Kramer & K. S. Cook (Eds.), *Trust and distrust in organizations* (pp. 189–213). New York: Russel Sage Foundation.

Mintzberg, H. (1983). *Structure in fives: Designing effective organizations*. Englewood Cliffs: Prentice-Hall.

Normann, R. (1977). *Management for growth*. Chichester: Wiley.

Shoham, A. (1998). Export performance: A conceptualization and empirical assessment. *Journal of International Marketing, 6*(3), 59–81.

Troy, K. (1994). *Change management: Strategic alliances*. Report No.1090-94-RR. New York: The Conference Board.

Welch, D. E., Welch, L. S., Wilkinson, I. F., & Young, L. C. (1996). Network analysis of a new export grouping scheme: The role of economic and non-economic relations. *International Journal of Research in Marketing, 13*(5), 463–477.

Welch, D. E., Welch, L. S., Young, L. C., & Wilkinson, I. F. (1998). The importance of networks in export promotion: Policy issues. *Journal of International Marketing, 6*(4), 66–82.

Wernerfelt, B. (1984). A resource-based view of the firm. *Strategic Management Journal, 5*(2), 171–180.

Wilkinson, I. F., & Mattsson, L. G. (1994). Trade promotion policy from a network perspective: The case of Australia. In: *10th Industrial Marketing & Purchasing Conference,* Groningen. (*Working paper 1/1993*, Department of Marketing, University of Western Sydney, Nepean).

Zou, S., & Stan, S. (1998). The determinants of export performance: A review of the empirical literature between 1987 and 1997. *International Marketing Review, 15*(5), 333–356.

Conclusions 6

In this book we have shed light on the role of export consortia and the key factors affecting successful cooperation among SMEs. The empirical analysis of nine export consortia promoted by UNIDO in Morocco, Tunisia, Peru and Uruguay between 2004 and 2007 shows that export consortia can be effective vehicles in assisting SMEs to overcome major barriers to international expansion. Although the consortia covered by our analysis are still in the initial stages of their life-cycle, empirical evidence confirms that they can play an important role in fostering the success of SMEs in developing countries and, as a result, the international competitiveness of these countries.

International expansion is increasingly seen as an essential means to enhance the economic growth of developing countries. However, such an opportunity is not simple to exploit. SMEs generally suffer from a number of barriers to export related to limitations of resources and capabilities. In developing economies in particular, SMEs cannot count on a favourable economic environment. In addition, given their unsophisticated domestic markets, SMEs in developing countries are unaccustomed to strong competition and satisfying demanding customers, conditions which are characteristic of developed markets.

Networking may be one way for small firms to overcome barriers to international expansion. Through networks firms can pool resources and competences in order to compete with rival foreign firms effectively and meet the needs of international customers. However, when firms are very small, networking is not a simple strategy. For micro and small firms it is almost impossible to become involved in alliances which are demanding in terms of resources and organizational skills (this is the case, for example, of joint ventures). Less binding forms of cooperation are therefore necessary.

Export consortia suit the needs of SMEs for a number of reasons. They require relatively little investment and can be managed in such a way that partners need only participate in those initiatives which are of real interest to them. Consortia are organized loosely enough to allow partners to define strategies autonomously.

Forming horizontal ties with other domestic partners may therefore enable firms to solve a variety of internal export problems concerning the completeness and quality of the value proposition, organizational and financial issues, and a lack of information about foreign markets.

Our analysis highlights the fact that SMEs benefit greatly from their participation in export consortia. Greater knowledge of foreign markets, a better reputation with international customers, participation in trade fairs that were previously inaccessible to individual firms and development of new business contacts abroad are some of the positive results reported by firms.

Empirical evidence also shows that the benefits of cooperation are not limited to the capacity to compete abroad. Although export consortia are networks for promoting internationalization, they also foster the development of intangible assets that help member firms to increase their competitiveness in their domestic markets. Beyond promoting export, a further strategic objective thus becomes increasingly important and, in some cases, dominant: upgrading and strengthening the organizational and managerial structure of member firms. This is particularly true in developing countries where firms are characterized by less managerial expertise and fewer organizational resources and staff than their counterparts in developed countries. An increase in 'relational capital' is a major result which can be exploited at home as well as abroad.

The experience of export consortia suggests an important implication for policy-makers who may be interested in setting up appropriate systems of incentives and support services that can enable firms to grow and be successful in foreign markets. When designing incentives and programmes that aim at fostering the competitiveness of SMEs, policy-makers should take into account the fact that, as well as financial and technical resources, relational capital is also crucial for greater competitiveness at both domestic and international level.

Another implication emerging from our analysis concerns the key role of network facilitators for successful cooperation among SMEs. Export consortia of SMEs are usually created via the initiative of third parties. Network facilitators promote and strengthen trust-based relationships among firms and provide a clear strategy for the alliance. In developing countries – where local environments usually have limited resources and few self-organized initiatives – this role is even more important and may be filled by special government agencies, specialized development banks, non-governmental organizations or multilateral international agencies (such as UNIDO). In the export consortia covered by our analysis, UNIDO played the role of network facilitator. In some cases, UNIDO worked in collaboration with local public institutions.

The role played by UNIDO goes far beyond supporting the initiatives of individual member firms, but is highly important at all stages of the consortium life-cycle, from the selection of member firms to the setting-up of the organizational structure and governance mechanisms. Financial support can be a strong incentive for inter-firm cooperation. However, this may not be sufficient to guarantee the survival of export consortia in the long term. As the experience of the nine consortia analyzed in the book shows, managerial, rather than merely financial, support from local institutions and international organizations is vital for the creation and success of this type of network. Managerial support can help firms increase their

6 Conclusions

cooperative skills and develop relational competences, as well as obtain financial resources. For example, in the cases studied here, UNIDO encouraged collaboration between the consortia and the public institutions which finance most of the consortia activities. The benefit of such support is important for two reasons. Firstly, member firms receive financial resources and, secondly, they develop relationships and competences which may be leveraged in the future, beyond even the 'network facilitator' support period.

Network facilitators play a fundamental role in enhancing trust-based relationships between partners, which are in turn central for the success of any alliance. Frequent and open communication and interactions both among member firms and towards external players are, in fact, necessary elements for the successful development of joint projects and activities, and the sharing of business ideas and resources.

This study also highlights important implications for entrepreneurs, managers and consultants who are interested in increasing the performance of export consortia. Our analysis shows that six areas are critical for the successful management of cooperation:

- *Managing the strategic alignment of member firms*: The strategic alignment of member firms must be assessed at the time the partners are selected and then continuously monitored at every stage of the consortium life-cycle.
- *Formulating consortium strategy*: The strategies of the export consortia studied here were at least partially formalized. UNIDO consultants emphasized the importance of developing a business plan for the consortium in order to help partners share ideas concerning the mission and future of the network. Business planning can be a very useful activity for building consensus among partners, clarifying the basic business idea of the venture and identifying gaps and financial requirements.
- *Designing the organizational structure*: The organizational structures of export consortia may be represented as a *continuum* ranging from a 'light' structure, where the consortium has little or no dedicated staff and resources, and all of the responsibilities and tasks are distributed among the individual firms, to a 'heavy' structure where several strategic activities are delegated to the consortium by member firms and the consortium can therefore call on more significant resources.
- *Leveraging on strategic resources and competences*: The competitiveness of export consortia depends on the set of strategic resources and distinctive capabilities developed and distributed at both consortium and member-firm level. The benefits of consortia are particularly significant in terms of development of intangible resources and relational capital.
- *Enforcing corporate governance and leadership*: The governance structure and mechanisms of the consortia also play a critical role in enhancing the strategic alignment of member firms and promoting their commitment. Defining the governance system primarily implies designing effective top-level management bodies and ensuring real participation of each member firm in the

strategy-making process and control over all decisions and actions implemented by the consortium.
- *Measuring consortium performance*: Measuring the performance of an export consortium is by no means a simple task. Consortium performance must be seen as a multi-dimensional construct. In a broader sense, the advantages for member firms are not limited to financial and market-based performance, but also include a number of additional benefits in terms of greater learning outcomes, increased reputation, higher relational capital and innovation. The advantages for member firms relating to all these areas should be continuously assessed.

Given the short life of the nine consortia studied, it is not possible to draw exhaustive conclusions about either the evolution of the specific organizational and strategic needs of export consortia over time or how to manage such consortia from a more dynamic perspective. Studying these consortia over a longer time period via a longitudinal analysis would provide empirical evidence of the changes which take place over the life-cycle of a consortium.

Further research should examine consortia at a more mature stage in order to shed light on patterns of consortium development and the key factors affecting long-term success. There are, therefore, a number of 'open issues' which need to be addressed.

However, on the basis of our analysis of export consortia, several ideas may be developed about how, and to what extent, third parties, such as network facilitators, can influence the success of these networks. In particular, we feel there are issues surrounding the timing of support given by third parties, the nature of the support that should initially be provided, and the kind of resources they should primarily be contributing.

As far as the timing of support is concerned, a period of approximately 5 to 6 years would appear to be compatible with the objective of supporting SMEs in developing their own capabilities to ensure the long-term autonomous survival of the consortium. Consortia which are heavily supported by third parties over a longer period risk becoming subsidized organizations and the entrepreneurial spirit and initiatives of the small entrepreneurs may be constrained. Firms involved in the development of export consortia should be aware from the outset of the temporary support they will receive from the network facilitator. Such awareness should contribute to motivating the consortium member firms to develop their capabilities and competences in terms of alliance management.

Regarding the nature of the support supplied by the network facilitator, two phases may be identified: (a) project development and partner selection, and (b) implementation. During the first phase, support from the external facilitators should focus primarily on helping member firms to achieve a strong strategic alignment and jointly define a common strategy. We can label this 'entrepreneurial support'. In the implementation phase, 'managerial support' is more important, as members of consortia need to develop management systems, structures, and values which are essential for long-term growth. Institutions that support the start-up and development of consortia should therefore be conscious of the need to adopt a more 'entrepreneurial' approach in the first stage, and a more 'managerial' one in the second stage.

Finally, if we look at the kind of resources that should be developed through the contribution of external support, our empirical analysis shows that such a contribution is highly significant in the area of intangible resources, in particular 'relational capital'. Relationships are crucial not only between member firms, but also outside them, i.e. in terms of links with public institutions. Only by leveraging on the exchanges of knowledge, information and opportunities within both the network and the supporting institutions in their domestic environment will SMEs increase their chances of success in international markets.

In addition, by developing stronger connections among small firms, export consortia can, at a domestic level, become the building blocks of a modern and dynamic business environment, open to international markets. In this way, they will be able to contribute effectively to the development of the home country.

Printed by Publishers' Graphics LLC USA
MO20120323-088
2012